MW01715521

THE POWERBOATERS' BIBLE

NOVA
Wellcraft

THE POWERBOATERS' BIBLE

By Mark Penzer

A completely revised edition of the book formerly entitled The Motorboatman's Bible

1977

DOUBLEDAY & COMPANY, INC., GARDEN CITY, NEW YORK

"Come to Champlain" (An Inland Cruise) by Mark Penzer reprinted by permission of *Motor Boating* magazine.

Library of Congress Cataloging in Publication Data
Penzer, Mark.
The powerboaters' bible.
Published in 1966 under title: The motorboatman's bible.
Includes index.
1. Motor-boats. I. Title.
GV835.P43 1977 797.1'25
ISBN 0-385-12669-7
Library of Congress Catalog Card Number 76-42427

COPYRIGHT © 1966, 1978 BY MARK PENZER
ALL RIGHTS RESERVED
PRINTED IN THE UNITED STATES OF AMERICA

(*Photo by the author.*)

To Eileen with love

This book has sold consistently well over the ten years that have passed since I wrote it. Many things have changed since then, affecting both the book—new laws, prices, addresses, new almost everything except concepts—and me. I was editor-in-chief of a boating magazine then, and a substantial portion of my life revolved around boats and boating; now I practice law, and a substantial portion of my life concerns contracts and wills and trials, though I have not lost my yen for the sea. Still, when the publisher asked me to take on a revision I procrastinated interminably over it. Shortly before my wife died, in September 1975, however, she had me promise her I would complete it. I should, she said, not for the money but because readers deserved the best I could give them. That's how she was, and in part it is why I continue to dedicate this book to her, Eileen, with love.

Mark Penzer
Dix Hills, New York
May 1976

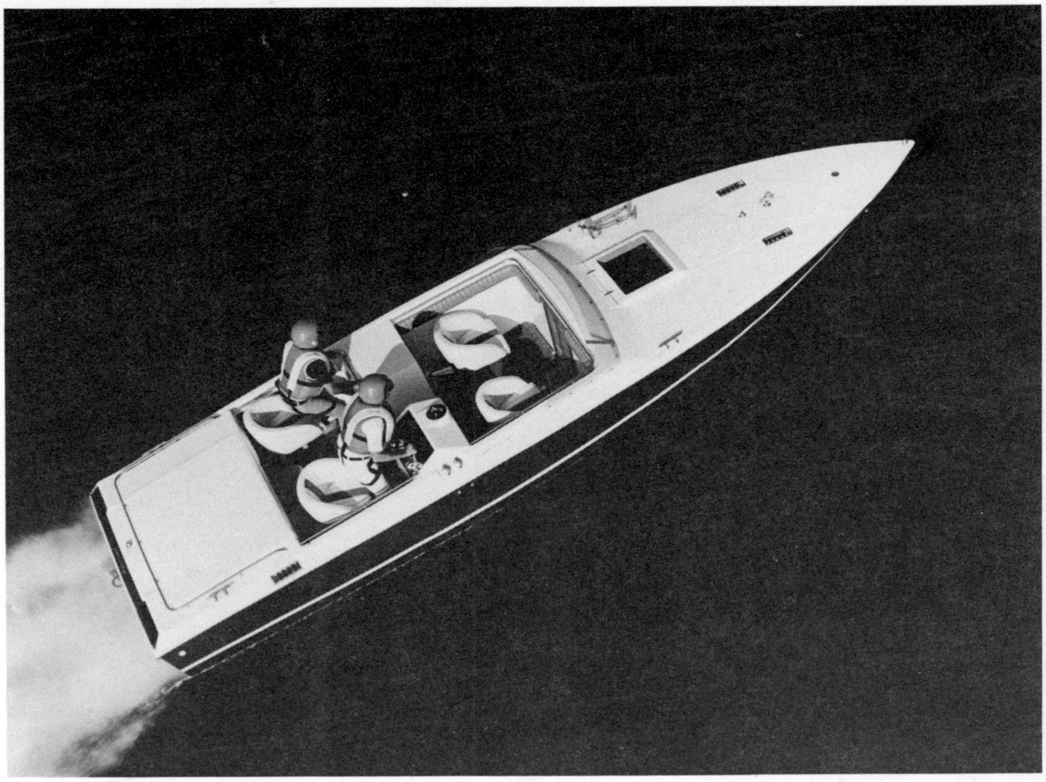

EVINRUDE

CONTENTS

(*Photos by the author.*)

THE POWERBOATERS' BIBLE

(*Photo by the author.*)

Chapter 1
TYPECASTING THE POWERBOAT

By law a powerboat is any watercraft no more than 65 feet long and equipped with propulsion machinery. That swallows a sizable chunk. For our purposes it is more helpful to break "powerboat" down into basic, broad types, zeroing in on the essence of each, those characteristics by which the type is known. Someone, count on it, will point out an example that is not within the boundaries I have laid for it. Such examples exist. But they are outdated or too much the exception to make their inclusion practical in this book.

Too, there are some classifications omitted from the analysis that follows. Houseboats, for one, and ski boats and hydroplanes and a few more I can think of quite readily. They do not appear because they are really specialized offshoots of the types treated. A houseboat, you see, is a kind of *cruiser,* or *motor yacht* if large enough, designed for more permanent living aboard and for running in shallower, better protected waters than is the conventional cruiser. Ski boats, which are speedy, compact craft usually fitted out with tow rings in the transom and an observer's seat facing aft, and hydroplanes, which are designed and powered to thump out incredible water speeds, are merely modifications of the basic *runabout*. Thus I have felt it unnecessary to examine all the strains. Photographs throughout this book, however, have been included with an eye toward exposing the wide variety of boats being built.

Runabout

This is an open, smallish (14 to 20 feet or so) boat, frequently fitted with a Navy top (folding canvas), or a solid one-piece top that on some models slides out of the way aft. Often the boat has a tiny forward compartment in which gear can be stowed, for room when you are under way and for safekeeping when you leave the boat. The runabout is not suitable for genuine cruising, having neither the size nor the facilities for it. It is, however, capable of sizzling speed, rendering the craft ideal for calm-water hops, for use as a towboat for water skiing, for a diving platform, for local fishing, and for scooting home in a

Houseboat is a kind of cruiser. This one is Boatel's 47-footer with fiberglass hull and a pair of 250-hp inboards.

Hydroplane is a kind of utility boat, all muscle and no frills (*Photo by the author.*)

Pontoon boat is another kind of utility, a floating patio that can be fun in calm waters. This model is built by Kayot with aluminum pontoons.

Runabout: Fiberglass, jet-powered 20-footer by Glastron/Carlson.

hurry when clouds make up menacingly in the distance. Although power can be inboard, stern- or jet-drive (see Chapter 3), most runabouts are outboard powered. For its size and intended use the runabout is well equipped to provide comfort and convenience. Some models have cockpit seats that fold down into "bunks," fit for sunning if not sleeping.

Utility

Commonly this is a nearly naked version of the runabout, the least expensive model in a builder's line, his runabout stripped fairly clean. Because the hull is identical to the runabout's, properly powered it too is a fast boat, capable of the variety of uses to which the runabout is put—but with less comfort, less trim. When economy is crucial, and a small, all-around boat is what you are after, the utility is the answer, since by simply adding equipment as budget and desire dictate you convert it from duckling to swan. Besides the essential equipment (see Chapter 6), however, don't launch without a windshield and a top. The windshield—be sure it is shatter-

Runabout: Fiberglass, outboard-powered 17-footer by Chrysler.

Runabout: Larson's Commander has 21-foot fiberglass hull, stern-drive power.

Runabout: Open bow section 18-footer by Silverline has stern-drive, 3-position reclining seats.

Runabout: Meant for bass fishing (see raised fishing seats forward and aft), this 15-footer by MFG comes well equipped including the wiring to hook up an electric trolling motor forward.

proof; too many are not—will divert wind and spray so you can see where you are going. The top will keep you from broiling beneath the sun and becoming bone-drenched in a drizzle.

Cruiser

Any powerboat can be a cruiser if it possesses the basic facilities for overnight accommodations. By definition, however, a cruiser has a cabin, hence the phrase "cabin cruiser" is a redundancy. It also has sleeping facilities, which may be V-berths fitted into the bow; pipe berths along either side of the boat; a dinette that converts into what is glibly called a double bed but which often is a bunk and a

Runabout: The 20-foot 4-inch Outrage by Boston Whaler has enough foam flotation in its hulls to make the craft virtually unsinkable.

half; a convertible sofa; or a full-size bed, box spring, thick mattress, and all. Two more items complete the cabin ingredients, a head and a galley.

The head, which is called a toilet, lavatory, or powder room in other circles, can be a completely private, spacious arrangement with shower, sinks, hot and cold water, vanity, electrically driven plumbing, and mosaic tiling. It can also be simply a john, discreetly concealed beneath, say, a hinged portion of a bunk and around which something like a shower curtain is drawn.

Galleys run the gamut also, from a diminutive icebox and two-burner alcohol stove to an all-stainless complex of gas or electric stove, oven, refrigerator, dishwasher, and deep-freeze, and yards of working counter space.

Finally, the cruiser has adequate tankage for fuel and fresh water, affording self-sufficiency for, at a minimum, a couple of back-to-back cruising days.

Cruiser sizes begin at about 22 feet—sometimes powered by outboards if the hull is small—and extend up to an indefinite length, though beyond 50 feet they frequently are termed motor yachts. Two variations on the cruiser theme are the "sedan cruiser" and the "express cruiser." The sedan cruiser is identified by its extra-long cabin structure, built with plenty of glass area so that the interior is bright and airy, and a minimum of 6 feet headroom throughout. Cabin length is achieved at the expense of cockpit area, so that the sedan cruiser is suited especially for cruising and "inside living" and not, for in-

Popular runabout features (besides the lady) are reclining seats—these are in a Glasspar hull—and (below) fixed back-to-back seats as in this 16-foot Chris-Craft.

Flat and fiberglass, this deck boat by Viking makes a handy platform for fishing, diving, or partying.

Utility: Small outboard-powered racing rigs—this one is a 12-footer—are good for only one thing. But they do move! Model here hits more than 125 miles per hour.

Utility: Classically what one thinks of under the heading of utility are these: a shell of a boat with a couple of kids hoping for trout and a small trolling motor astern (boat is Lowe Industries' 12-foot aluminum pram); or a workboat like this 14-foot aluminum Monark.

Utility: Plenty of fishing room characterizes this 19-foot 6-inch fiberglass Aquasport powered by a 140-hp MerCruiser stern-drive. Cuddy (small enclosed space forward) provides stowage room.

Utility: Another fast fiberglass fishing rig is this 23-foot Mako with inboard power, center console steering, and a fish well in the stern.

Cruiser: F-28 is model designation of Trojan's 28-foot sedan cruiser cleverly designed to afford accommodations below generally found only on larger sedans. Included are upper and lower berths, plenty of stowage areas, and a 12-foot 3-inch beam (width).

stance, for fishing. The express-cruiser tag implies not some particular layout but speed, greater than what is expected of similarly proportioned cruisers. Unfortunately these two terms, sedan cruiser and express cruiser, are regularly bandied about in advertisements without regard for their meanings. Look closely to see what you are getting.

Day cruiser

Intended primarily for fishing rather than voyaging or extended living aboard, the type is a modification of the true cruiser, skimping in or completely devoid of one or more of the cruiser elements enumerated above. Hardest hit are sleeping accommodations, since fresh water, toilet facilities, ample fuel, and a galley are as welcome for fishing as for cruising. The galley need not be extensive, since time spent continuously aboard will be relatively brief. Berths may be provided but these will be minimal, to occupy as little space as possible. The day cruiser is sometimes called a "weekender," implying with commendable candor that one can probably endure a night or two aboard but not much more.

Sportfisherman

This term can apply to any boat from utility to cruiser. The heart of the label is that the boat is fitted out particularly with fishing in mind, probably deep-sea fishing but not necessarily. It may or may not have cruising facilities; it may be starkly functional or luxuriously so; it may be designed for both cruising and fishing. There is a distinct trend toward restricting the term to boats 30 feet and longer that do have cruising facilities, a flying bridge (a place to sit and steer, situated above cabin-top level), a cockpit large enough for at least one fighting chair and possibly more, a fish-well at the transom in which the catch can be stowed until fetching shore, a gin pole (hoist) to boat the big ones, and possibly a compartmented locker or two for reels, lures, hooks, sinkers, and so on. To this the owner will add a tuna tower, outriggers, a bow pulpit if swordfish is on his agenda, gaffs, a fish finder, and a great deal of hope.

Cruiser: Sport Cruiser is model name of this 31-footer by AMF-Hatteras. It sleeps six, comes with hydraulic steering and automatic fire-control system. Hardware is stainless steel.

Cruiser: Trawler-type 34-foot Marine Trader has fiberglass hull, 120-hp fresh-water cooled diesel with 300-gallon fuel tanks for 1,000-mile cruising range. She's built in Taiwan, sold in U.S.

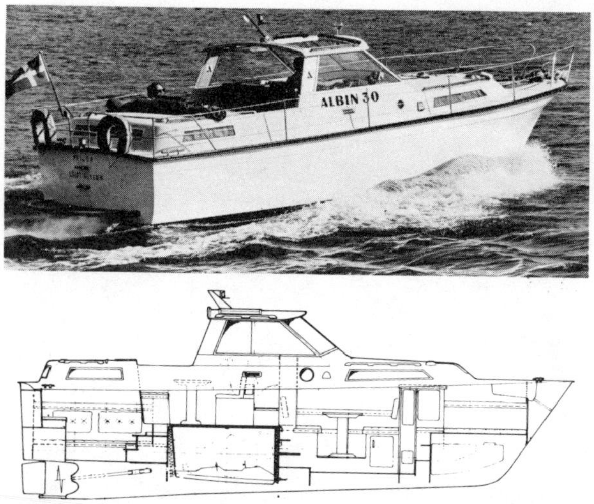

Cruiser: Another trawler type, the 30-foot Albin, has 130-hp Perkins diesel (which should eat some 3 gph while providing about 15 knots) and a 300-mile range. Sleeping accommodations are for six (see layout drawing) with two forward, two on convertible dinette, and two in aft stateroom. Boat is built in Sweden.

Cruiser: Part houseboat (superstructure), part conventional cruiser (hull) is Boatel's 40-foot Bluewater. Options include a bathtub.

Motor yacht

Here one deals with Sumptuous Yachting, which smacks of leisure, comfort, and wealth. Like mansions, motor yachts come in all forms but have at least the following characteristics in common. Their length is 50 feet and up, they are capable of long offshore cruises (large fuel and water tanks), and each department—galley, navigating, lounging—is punctuated with virtually every marine accessory available, especially electronic ones. The yacht has two or more separate staterooms; quarters, traditionally forward, for at least one paid hand; a deckhouse (steering or helmsman station), probably a lounging salon, and a generator to produce enough shoreside-like electricity to operate most of the accessories wherever the yacht is. The power plant is almost sure to be a twin-screw setup, which is to say it will have two separate engines driving two propellers.

Motor sailer

Theoretically the motor sailer is an impartial descendant of motorboat and sailboat, half one, half the other. Most models, however, are custom built and wind up, if not preponderantly power or sail, visibly leaning to one or the other. When they are primarily power, sails are bent on to preserve fuel or to provide a steadying influence when the wind whistles up. When they are primarily sail, power is used to continue on course in a toothless breeze, to negotiate busy anchorages and tricky marina slips, or simply to make haste when the hour drags.

Auxiliary

When under power, the auxiliary is deemed a powerboat, subject to the appropriate rules of the road. For all other practical purposes, however, auxiliaries are sailboats, a fact that accounts for their meager treatment in this book. What distinguishes the auxiliary from the other sailboats is its possession of an engine, however small. As a rule, the engine is horsepowered enough to provide only easy-gaited headway for harbors, berthing, and no-wind or low-wind conditions.

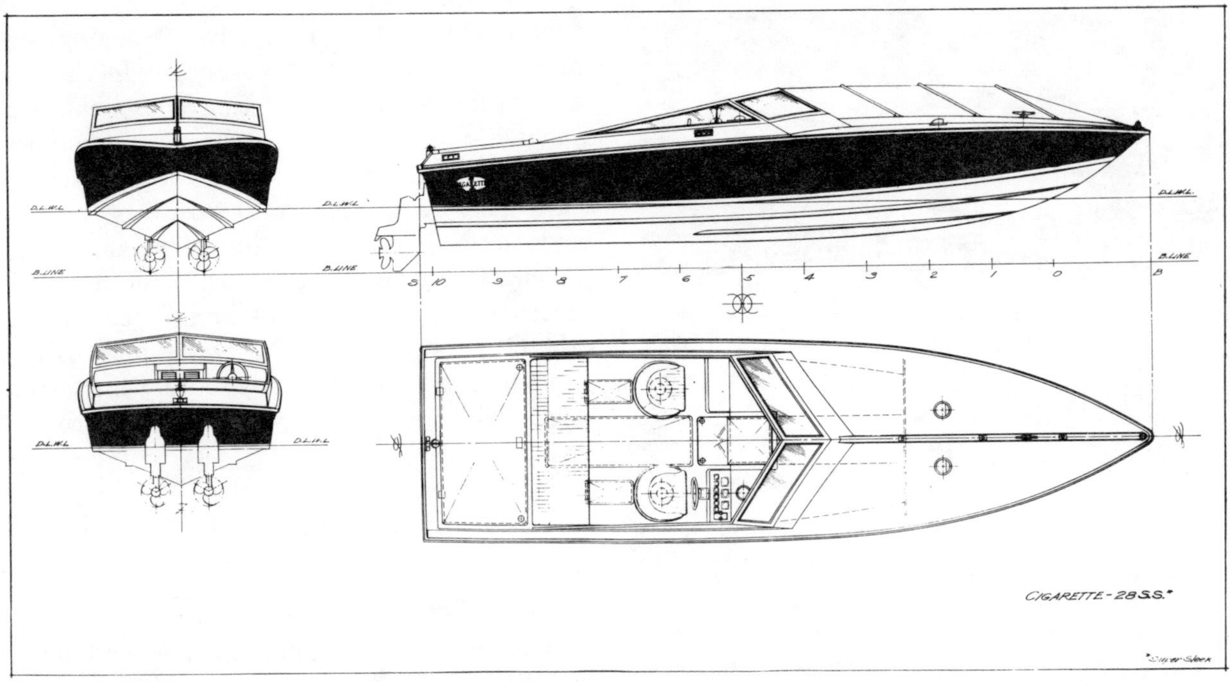

Racing cruiser: Cigarette 28-SS is posh, fast (70 mph is fast!), and expensive (up to $30,000 depending on power chosen). Twin bunks are forward, as is the head. To be fair, this might be better listed as a runabout with bunks, but whatever, she's ideal for racing, coastal patrol (for which Israel has purchased a few), and showing off around the yacht club.

Cruiser: Double cabin 36-foot sedan cruiser by Uniflite has fiberglass hull, teak trim, is available in a variety of layouts. Standard power is a pair of 350-hp gasoline engines.

Day cruiser: The 21-foot Bonanza by Cruisers/Mirro Marine can be had in outboard or stern-drive models.

Day cruiser: Chris-Craft calls it the Overnighter. She's 23 feet 1 inch down the centerline and 8 feet in beam (a popular width because more requires a special permit to trail on Interstate Highways).

Day cruiser: Dyer Offshore Bass Boat, built by the Anchorage, is 28 feet 6 inches overall, can be had with gas or diesel power. Hull is fiberglass.

Express cruiser: Bertram's 35-footer has twin 350-hp gas inboards, 35-mph speeds, and a fuel capacity of 285 gallons. Beam is 13 feet.

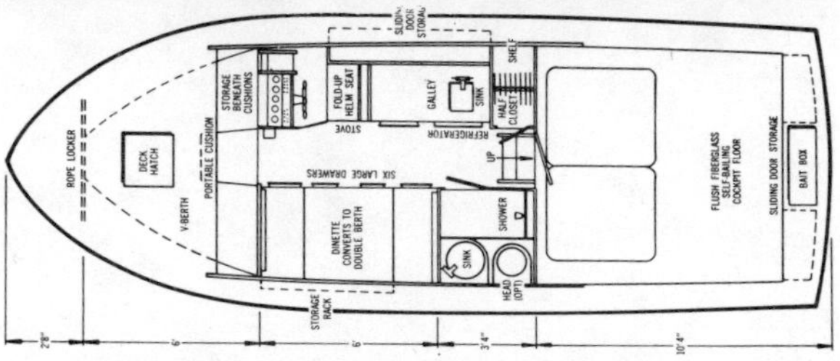

Express cruiser: The implication is speed. The Santa Cruz is Carver's 28-footer, available with twin 230-hp inboards.

Sportfisherman: Cobia Caribbean is 23 feet 9 inches long, can handle a pair of 200-hp outboards. Fishing gear on this rig includes spotting tower, outriggers, and fighting chair.

Sportfisherman: Hatteras 46-footer was most expensive boat at '76 National Boat Show at $173,600. She has two heads, air conditioning, stereo, and a pair of GM diesels. Fuel capacity is 650 gallons.

Sportfisherman: Tournament Fisherman by Chris-Craft is 45 feet 6 inches long, comes with a pair of 320-hp diesels. Her price tag: about $143,000.

Motor yacht: Wooden-hulled Florencia is Grebe-built 65-footer with diesel power.

Motor yacht: Burger Boats built the 96-foot Shangri-La. Hull is aluminum.

Motor sailer: Mostly sail is this steel-hulled Dutch-built 41-footer, C'est Bon.

Motor sailer: Mostly power is Admiral Blake, a Stonington-built 50-footer. Small sail is used to help steady the boat when wind kicks up.

Auxiliary: Essentially the craft is a sailboat but with a small motor to help when there's no wind or in crowded harbors.

Double-ender: Pointed both forward and aft, these able craft are popular with Coastguardsmen and whaleboatmen.

Hydrofoils are a sort of hull on stilts. The advantage of a hydrofoil craft is that with less hull in the water there's less resistance, and the craft can travel faster cheaper. Its future is in the commuter business.

Amphibians: Every so often someone tries to market a seagoing car—this was the 14-foot Amphicar—but none yet has been commercially successful. The Amphicar relied on its wheels as rudders, was difficult to control.

Inflatables: Making a noticeable dent in the low-cost end of boating—this 12-foot 3-inch Avon model sells for $700—are the inflatables, made mostly out of synthetics such as nylon.

Oddball boats, while we're on the subject, include the scooter boats such as this 10-foot Streaker manufactured by Chris-Craft. For safety's sake, add a "dead-man's throttle," a device that automatically closes the throttle if the driver is thrown overboard.

Chapter 2
A BUYING APPROACH

Why bother with boat types? Because if you are about to buy a boat, knowing them will sharpen your hunt and save you time, frustration, and (possibly) money. Boat type, in fact, is the first decision to make, even before price, size, and brand are settled. There is nothing difficult about choosing once you familiarize yourself with the definitions given in the preceding chapter. Types are designed for particular uses. Your job is to match the type with the use to which you will put the boat in the waters you expect to ply.

I have qualified "use" by the "waters you expect to ply" for an important reason: the physical conditions in which your boat will operate may preclude choosing a type which would otherwise be the best bet. If, for example, most of your running is to consist of short sprints, with perhaps two or three persons aboard, a utility or a runabout, depending on how much money you want to spend initially, is best suited for the chore. That is what utilities and runabouts are for. But if the running is to be done on open waters—along the coasts, for example, or on any of the Great Lakes—and if your boating season is too brief to permit the luxury of boating only on still days with flat water, you need much more boat. You need more draft (depth in the water) for stability, more freeboard (height of the hull from the waterline up) for protection from breaking seas, more weight to avoid being bobbed and pitched. Probably a day cruiser is what you need.

If, to take another example, you plan to do a lot of extended overnighting afloat, a cruiser is certainly your answer. But suppose the waters you plan generally to cruise are shoal, like Chesapeake Bay in Maryland or Barnegat Bay in New Jersey? A conventional cruiser—probably the one you are contemplating—may present too much draft for you to want to contend with; it may make cruising impossible, as where the draft is greater than the water's depth, or annoyingly burdensome, as where draft and depth are so close that continuous steering care is necessary to avoid going aground. This is a demanding strain on the helmsman. Look for a type with less draft: a houseboat, perhaps, or at least a shoal-draft cruiser.

The type-selection process, then, is one of

compromise. First find the *ideal* boat type. Then weigh its characteristics against the particular physical conditions it must face. If you have to compromise, lean toward satisfying the conditions; these you cannot change.

The shapes they're in

The reason I have led into choosing boat type before considering hull shape is that most competent boat designers are as ready to use one shape as the other, V-bottom or round-bottom. With the exception of some scows, the flat bottom is found principally on rowboats and prams (a rowboat with a blunt bow) and so will not be considered here.

A round-bottom hull is one in which the sides of the boat *curve* to the bottom; a V-bottom, one in which the sides and bottom meet at an angle. The joint or point where they meet is called the "chine." This explains why V-bottom boats are sometimes referred to as "hard-chined" boats—the bottom makes a "hard" turn from the sides. Technically speaking, I suppose the round-bottom hull has no chine, but it is often called a "soft-chined" boat.

The angle produced by the hard chine—the amount of vee in a V-bottom—is called "deadrise." In the past the V-bottom boat usually had its least deadrise aft, at the transom, increasing gradually as it approached the bow. Viewing the bottom from astern, you would see a flat or almost flat bottom beneath the transom, steepening into a deeper and deeper V as you look farther forward. This flat aftersection produces the *planing* surface on which boats with adequate power are able to skim over, or plane, the surface of the water. Boats which run *through* the water, instead of over its top, are called displacement boats and are almost always larger, heavier, and slower than planing boats.

There is a growingly discernible trend toward carrying the deadrise uniformly aft along the length of the hull rather than toward flattening it out aft, even on planing boats. Constant deadrise, the theory is, sets up less water resistance than a hull with varying deadrise (and so requires less power to be moved as quickly).

The niceties of the subject, I think, are beyond the layman's grasp. But that should not disturb you. If the design is true and the construction right, I doubt if much consideration should be given to whether the boat is round-bottomed or V-bottomed with variable or constant deadrise. Each shape can be—indeed, *has* been—used to produce a thoroughly efficient design. That is why I have suggested you choose boat type without being influenced by bottom shape. To dispel some clouds that hover over the subject, however, let's analyze the pet notions you are bound to hear sooner or later.

V-bottom hulls are faster than round-bottom hulls

True generally, but in low-speed boats the round bottom offers less water resistance and so can be propelled more easily. At moderate speeds performance depends more on major hull particulars—location of the center of gravity, beam at the transom, running lines, for example—than on whether the hull is round or V. For high speeds the V-bottom has the greater capability.

V-bottom hulls are drier than round-bottom hulls

Not necessarily. In a head sea (waves approaching from forward of the boat) the cockpit will stay about as dry on a good round-bottom boat as on a good V-bottom boat. If each is poorly designed the V-bottom boat, true, will stay drier, but it will pound more than the round-bottom vessel. In a following sea (waves approaching from astern) the old-time round-bottom boats tended to broach (turn broadside to the waves) more than did V-bottoms. Modern design and the effective placement of spray rails has greatly thwarted this

V-bottom, as on this Formula fiberglass hull, meets boat sides at abrupt angle forming what are called the "chines."

Round bottom—this one is on a wooden Richardson hull—curves into boat sides. Such hulls are sometimes called "soft-chined" boats.

tendency so that both types respond similarly in following-sea conditions.

Round-bottom hulls are more seaworthy

Not so. Seaworthiness depends more on the strength of the structure and its over-all design than on its V or round qualities.

Round-bottom hulls are tippy

Yes and no. Given the same weight, same beam at the waterline, and same center-of-gravity location, the round-bottom and the V-bottom boat will possess about the same *initial* stability. If you step gently aboard each boat, each will heel about the same amount. Should you jump onto the gunwale (rhymes with tunnel and indicates the top of the hull's side), the round-bottom craft will heel more sharply than the V-bottom one. It will also roll more times before coming to rest, the shape of the V-bottom having a greater damping effect. In rough water the V-bottom should provide the more comfortable rolling motions, and this is generally true in coastal waters. On shoal bays, where wave lengths are short, the round-bottom boat is apt to be the more comfortable.

What will it cost you?

Presumably you have pinpointed the boat type you are after by now if you are following this chapter's buying scheme. The most difficult step is next: come up with a figure you can spend. Be realistic. Include in your calculations operating costs (food, fuel, and boat maintenance), insurance, dockage, winter storage if necessary, and repair—if nothing else, you will whack out a propeller now and then. Once you arrive at a figure, hold it; a struggle to meet stale bills takes the pleasure out of boating.

Although I cannot tell how much you are able to spend, I can indicate about how much you will have to. The prices that follow are 1976 figures for, in each case, popular makes of at least reasonably good quality. Prices, of course, vary regionally and with time, but the data here will at least serve as rough guides. The tag for outboard boats does not include power (but see "How Much for a Kicker?" following the boat price information); prices for inboard boats do include the standard engine. What other items are included as "standard" depends upon the make and size of the boat. I do not consider this element important, however, since, in one way or another, you pay for what you get.

How much for the boat?*

Outboards	
14′ Alumacraft utility (aluminum)	$ 469
14′ Ouachita utility (fiberglass)	998
16′2″ Mckenzie runabout (aluminum)	1,690
16′4″ Wellcraft runabout (fiberglass)	6,495

* Sources for prices given throughout this book were mostly boat dealers, obtained without disclosing my trade connections. Where it appeared possible to haggle, I haggled, but there was more potential for negotiating over accessories than hull price.

17′1″ Crestliner runabout (aluminum)	2,595
17′3″ Chrysler runabout (fiberglass)	2,580
18′2″ Smoker-Craft runabout (aluminum)	2,333
18′10″ MFG runabout (fiberglass)	3,600
19′6″ Aquasport utility (fiberglass)	3,795
20′4″ Grady-White day cruiser (fiberglass)	5,145
21′5″ Starcraft runabout (aluminum)	3,180
21′9″ Mako utility (fiberglass)	4,395
23′ Slickcraft utility (fiberglass)	6,480

Inboards

16′5½″ Correct Craft runabout, 225 hp (fiberglass)	5,450
18′1″ Glastron runabout, 455 hp (fiberglass)	8,000
21′6″ Riva runabout, 210 hp (wood)	21,900
23′1″ Chris-Craft runabout, 250 hp (fiberglass)	9,975
24′ Aquasport runabout, 250 hp (fiberglass)	10,700
25′10″ Pacemaker cruiser, 220 hp (fiberglass)	14,800
28′ Aluminum Cruisers cruiser, 225 hp (aluminum)	13,850
30′7″ Bertram cruiser, twin 225 hp (fiberglass)	25,300
32′3″ Stamas cruiser, twin 225 hp (fiberglass)	37,550
33′ Egg Harbor cruiser, twin 225 hp (fiberglass)	38,000
35′ Chris-Craft cruiser, twin 235 hp (fiberglass)	42,000
36′ Hatteras cruiser, twin 330 hp (fiberglass)	57,800
40′4″ Viking cruiser, twin 350 hp (fiberglass)	65,800
44′3″ Trojan motor yacht, twin 330 hp (fiberglass)	81,965
60′ Manson Motor Yacht, twin 350 hp (wood)	190,000
80′ Huckins Sport Fisherman, twin 650 hp (wood and fiberglass)	750,000

Kit Boats

Catalogs—enclose $1 for each one you want—are available from:

Clark Craft, 16 Aqua Lane, Tonawanda, N.Y. 14150; and Glen-L Marine Designs, 9152 Rosecrans Blvd., Bellflower, Calif. 90706.

Models in any stage of construction are available from:

Glass Craft Yachts, 2500 S. Susan St., Santa Ana, Calif. 92704 (models from 47′ to 65′).

Westwind Yachts, Naval Design Services, Inc., P.O. Box 19302, Sacramento, Calif. 95819 (models from 35′10″ to 43′10″).

Other suppliers of kit boats include:

Huck Finn, 105 Cambridge St., Minneapolis, Minn. 55432 (pontoon boats 13″ to 24″).

Luger Industries, 3800 West Highway 13, Burnsville, Minn. 55337 (fiberglass runabouts and cruisers from 17″ to 31′6″).

How much for a kicker?†

Gasoline

1.2 hp Tas, air cooled	$ 160
2 hp Evinrude	250
3 hp British Seagull	281
4.5 Mercury	480
5.5 hp Clinton, air cooled	280
6 hp Chrysler	530
7.5 hp Sears, Roebuck	250
7.5 Honda, four cycle	519
9.9 Johnson	715
10 hp Chrysler	715
15 hp Evinrude	785
25 hp Johnson	890
45 hp Chrysler, electric starting	1,230
50 hp Mercury, electric starting	1,670
70 hp Evinrude, electric starting	1,740

90 hp Chrysler, electric starting	1,935
115 hp Johnson, electric starting	2,115
135 hp Evinrude, electric starting	2,200
150 hp Mercury, electric starting	2,510
175 hp Mercury, electric starting	3,100
200 hp Evinrude, electric starting	2,950

Electric models are rated by voltage and amperage, not by horsepower. Manufacturers include: Evinrude Motors, 4143 N. 27th St., Milwaukee, Wis. 53216; The Eska Company, 2400 Kerper Blvd., Dubuque, Iowa 52001; Johnson Outboards, 299 Sea Horse Dr., Waukegan, Ill. 60085; Minn Kota Inc., 201 N. 17th St., Moorehead, Minn. 56560; and Pflueger Sporting Goods, 301 Ansin Blvd., Hallandale, Fla. 33009.

Before you buy, try

With type and budget determined, select the particular boat size or size range you want. Obviously price must influence this decision, but you may be able to acquire a larger boat by doing without some of the equipment or construction features on which you have set your sights. The best way—no, the *only* way—to learn if a boat is adequate in size is to *use* the craft under conditions that approximate those you will meet: similar waters, the same number of persons aboard, staying out as long as you will, doing those things you plan to do. Increasingly such a demonstration can be arranged with the boat dealer. If you are unable to do this, you may be able to charter (rent) a similar boat, perhaps an identical model, for as long as you like. Using it is the only way you will know.

With type, price, and size in hand, two factors remain, hull material and quality, or brand.

The stuff of which boats are made

The material from which boats have been fashioned for the longest time is wood. Steel, aluminum, and fiberglass-reinforced plastic (popularly snipped in speech to "fiberglass"), however, have made deep inroads, and roughly in that chronological order. Traditionalists will have nothing but wood; anything else "just doesn't look like a boat." (Fans of wood boats will be interested in The Wooden Boat Club, 92 Hickory Grove Dr., Larchmont, N.Y. 10538. Membership includes buying privileges and a quarterly magazine.)

There is no fair rebuttal to taste but it is, no one will deny, becoming increasingly difficult to find a new wood boat except in the custom-built field. Perhaps a meatier argument is made out by those who point to the universal familiarity with wood as a boatbuilding material. The gist of this logic is, "You can always find someone to fix it and, with centuries of experience to draw upon, fix it right." Furthermore some naval architects contend that no other material can as readily be turned to so fair a curve without losing needed strength, especially when the design is intricate or the balance delicate.

"Nonsense," say opposing camps, supporting their stands with laboratory tests, statistical data, and a not-inconsiderable number of successful boats built of the materials being championed.

The debate will endure for a long time to come, heightened no doubt by the appearance of still newer hull materials (ferrocement, for instance) and combinations of existing ones. I think no one can furnish a cleanly chiseled answer as to which material *is* best, though many pretend to. Each material has merit. Fiberglass requires less maintenance than wood. Wood does present the traditional "boaty" appearance besides possessing at least some of

† Unless otherwise indicated, models are two-cycle, water-cooled, and manually started.

the advantages claimed for it above. Aluminum provides strength at less weight than other presently usable boatbuilding materials, thus needing less power to be moved as quickly. Steel is durable and has great impact strength. Both metals, properly alloyed, finished, and tended, do resist rust.

If any one of these characteristics—the list is not exhaustive—is convincing enough to sway your choice, fine. In any case, look to the quality of the particular boat you are buying, whatever its material.

Pig in a poke

If you are not a seasoned skipper do not rush into a purchase; there are too many crummy boats around. The importance of actually using the boat you may buy has already been stressed. But without experience you will be unable to evaluate the vessel in terms of condition, relative performance, and safety. Get help. I recommend hiring a professional boat surveyor (for names write to the National Association of Marine Surveyors, P.O. Box 55, Peck Slip Station, New York, N.Y. 10038). For a fee that varies with the value of the boat, the distance he must travel, and the time he must spend, the surveyor will inspect the craft with scrupulous care, poking in corners for rot, cracked frames, inadequate ventilation, improper fastenings, and potential engine troubles, and otherwise earn his money twice over. It is a tidy investment for so real a risk, whether the boat be new or used.

I also recommend avoiding the advice of friends, however well-meaning they are or impressive their marine background. When word of your boat-shopping gets out, advice, as a rule, pours in and if heeded will at best confuse you. "Facts" will be drawn from personal experiences and tastes, seldom observed objectively enough to be of value to you. Get help, yes, but competent, professional, disinterested help.

There are collateral approaches. Read as much as you can about the kinds of boat you are considering (write to boating magazines and request tear sheets of whatever each has published on the boats you are interested in). Study brochures and advertisements closely and comparatively. Visit boat shows. And buy only from reputable sources.

Extreme caution is called for if you should buy your boat from a stranger who is neither dealer nor boat broker (nautical version of a used-car dealer). The condition of the boat can be learned, as has been said, by a marine surveyor; that is no problem. What is hard to learn is whether the seller representing himself as the owner of the boat is in fact its owner. Most pre-1963 boats do not have serial numbers; the numbers on those that do can be "doctored" with a pen knife or with putty and paint. And since, with certain exceptions that are not applicable here, one cannot transfer a greater interest than one has, you will not get title to a boat from someone who does not have title to give, your innocence and good faith notwithstanding. Try, as has been said, to buy from established, reputable sources—suable sources, should anything go wrong.

What about a used boat?

The most persuasive argument that can be mustered for buying a used rather than a new boat is that you can get more for your money. Almost always you will get more size—and more power, since the engine, unless the boat is older than six or seven years, is likely to be in keeping with the vessel's size. But will you get more value?

Sure. If the boat meets your needs. And if the boat is in sound enough shape to last awhile. Such models are hard to find—though not impossible. The best source is a boat broker. The better brokers count on your becoming a long-term customer, continually returning to trade up, and so, if for no other reason, they do not attempt to hustle you into an unhappy transaction. From what you tell him, the savvy broker will know just what boat is right for you—for your pocket and for your plans. He will insist (if he does not, you must) on making the sale depend on the outcome of a survey of the boat. For this survey you generally pay. For those defects that need to be repaired on the boat the seller generally pays, either directly or by decreasing the selling price accordingly. Boat brokers advertise in boating magazines, newspapers, and the Yellow Pages.

How much can you expect to save by buying a used boat?

There is no universally recognized blue book of boats as there is for cars, though at least one publisher, BUC International Corporation, 2455 E. Sunrise Blvd., Fort Lauderdale, Fla. 33304, is attempting to earn such recognition for its annual *Used Boat Directory*. The difficulty in establishing a used-boat price guide is that there is no clear, consistent relationship between what a given boat brought when new and what it commands now when used. Boats do not depreciate in market value the way automobiles do.

If dry rot has taken a strong hold (the wood will feel spongy to the touch; that is why surveyors poke around with the tip of a knife or a screwdriver), or if in general the boat has been badly maintained, it may have virtually no value though only a year or two old. If the boat has been scrupulously maintained and regally fitted out, the asking price may be close to the original price. Occasionally such a boat, when only a few of its kind have been built, brings an even higher price than it first sold for. But between these extremes fall most of the used boats a broker will agree to list; they are not unique and their condition is good (the hull may need paint and the engine a tune-up). With the help of about a dozen boat brokers across the country I have worked up a rough price guide for such used boats having moderate power and a conservative inventory of gear. Use the guide with a great deal of reservation, since among other factors place and time will *radically* affect its application.

How much for a used boat?

Years old	*Length*	*% less than original price*
same year	up to 36′	10 to 15
same year	37′ to 65′	10 to 20
1	up to 25′	20 to 25
1	26′ to 50′	20 to 33⅓
1	51′ to 65′	20 to 25
2 to 4	up to 25′	30 to 40
2 to 4	26′ to 36′	30 to 35
2 to 4	37′ to 65′	40 to 50
5 to 10	up to 25′	50 to 60
5 to 10	26′ to 50′	50 to 55
5 to 10	51′ to 65′	40 to 50

Some actual used-boat listings

19′ Sea Ray, 1973, 225 hp stern-drive	$4,500
21′ Donzi, 1974, 270 hp stern-drive	$9,500
25′ Carver, 1975, 233 hp stern-drive	$10,900
25′ Bertram, 1966, twin 165 hp stern-drives	$12,800
26′ Pacemaker, 1968, 250 hp (new 1972)	$5,495
31′ Uniflite, 1969, twin 225 hp	$22,950
34′ Drift-R-Cruise (houseboat), 1968, 225 hp	$9,000
36′ Trojan, 1972, 280 hp	$29,000
38′ Hatteras, 1970, twin diesels	$53,000
42′ Chris-Craft, 1971, twin 300 hp	$45,000
45′ Colonial, 1967, 300 hp (new 1976)	$39,900
50′ Glebe, 1968, twin diesels	$55,000

Breaking the Used-boat Code

Until you have had experience with classified used-boat ads you may have difficulty deciphering the jargon. The following glossary will help.

TS or T/S=twin screw, two engines.
SS or S/S=single screw, one engine; or stainless steel; or ship-to-shore radio.
I/O=inboard-outboard, or stern-drive, engine.
FWC=fresh water cooling.
DD=direct drive.
RG=reduction gear.
Gen.=generator.
SSB=single sideband radio.
VHF=very high frequency radio.
RDF=radio direction finder.
ADF=automatic radio direction finder.
FB or F/B=flying bridge.
FB sed.=sedan cruiser with flying bridge.
Bimini top=canvas awning usually over flying bridge and/or tuna tower.
Dual controls=two steering stations.
Fathometer=particular-brand depth finder often misused to denote any depth finder.

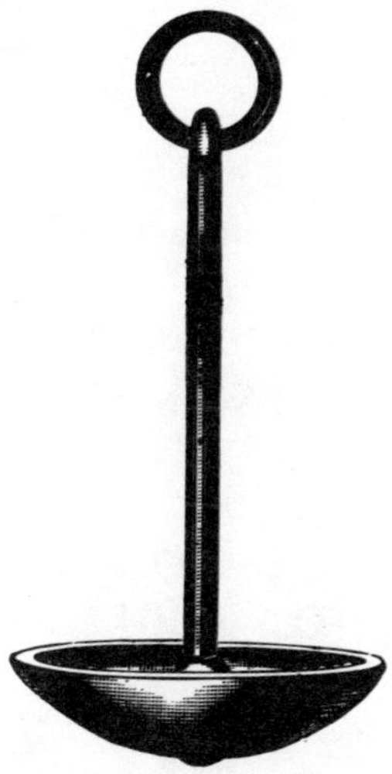

Typical mushroom anchor used to keep mooring buoy in place.

Used or new: Insure!

You are not compelled to insure your pleasure boat against damage or yourself against liability arising out of your boat ownership. Insurance is a gamble, no doubt about it: the gamble is that you will sustain losses in an amount greater than the cost of a covering policy. And it can be a poor gamble, because premiums are set so that the odds are stacked for the house. It is nevertheless worth the gamble. Besides assuring protection against losses in the future, insurance buys you peace of mind in the present.

If you do insure you can expect to pay about 4 to 7 per cent of the boat's total value for a marine insurance package. Rates are "negotiable," which is to say that your insurance agent can wheel and deal with various underwriters to get you the best price for identical coverage.

Berthing the boat

Unless you possess waterfront property you will likely keep your boat at a marina (rhymes with arena). Marina berthing charges vary according to demand for space and the overhead it must pay for. Usually the marina will offer you a choice of a slip or a mooring at which to keep your boat while she is afloat. Taking a slip means you can secure your boat alongside a pier (structure perpendicular to the shore) or wharf (structure parallel to the shore), either of which almost everyone calls a "dock." Technically this is incorrect; a dock is the water area between two piers, but I know only one boatman who insists on that usage. He is right, but lonely. Taking a mooring means you will leave your boat at anchor, generally within a few hundred feet off shore of the marina. The anchor, frequently the type that looks like an inverted mushroom and so is called a "mushroom anchor," is owned and put in place by the marina; a small buoy marks its location and keeps the anchor line (usually a chain) at the surface where you can grab it. The marina will assign a mooring for your exclusive use.

The convenience of a slip, as against a mooring, is attractive, and the difference in rates reflects this. At a slip you can come and go as you please; at a mooring you must use a dinghy (yours or the marina's) to ferry out

Characteristics of Boating Metals

Metal	*Composition*	*Tensile Strength per Square Inch*	*Characteristics in Boat Use*
Aluminum	Al‡ 92–99% Cu Mg Mn Si Fe 1–7%	13,000 to 55,000	Lightest of the metals. Strength of some alloys about equal to mild steel.
Copper	Cu 99.9% O .04%	35,000 to 45,000	Very resistant to corrosion. Relatively soft, malleable.
Brass (commercial bronze)	Cu 90% Zn 10%	45,000	Not much stronger than pure copper. Corrosion resistant.
Brass (naval bronze)	Cu 60–65% Zn 34–39% Sn ¾%	50,000 to 55,000	Resilient and tough. Developed by Navy to get higher corrosion resistance to salt.
Brass (yellow)	Cu 62–64% Zn 35–37%	55,000 to 60,000	Greater strength than mild carbon steel. Tough, malleable, rustproof. High corrosion resistance.
Silicon bronze (Everdur, etc.)	Cu 94–96% Si 2–3½% Zn 1–5% (None in Everdur)	70,000	High-strength, non-corrosive alloy, mostly made of copper.
Nickel alloys (Monel, etc.)	Ni 67–77% Cu 30% Fe 1.4%	82,000	Exceptional qualities of strength, versatility, and highest resistance to corrosion.
Stainless steel (austenitic group)	Cr 16–26% Ni 8–22%	90,000 to 124,000	Highly resistant to corrosion. Non-magnetic for all practical purposes. Very hard, strong.

‡ Symbols used in this column: Al, aluminum; Cr, chromium; Cu, copper; Fe, iron; Mg, magnesium; Mn, manganese; Ni, Nickel; O, oxygen; Si, silicon; Sn, tin; and Zn, zinc.

Marinas are where you berth your boat, but the lines for a season's spot are long. (*Photo by the author.*)

and back. At a slip you can unload or load the boat with ease; with a dinghy this is sometimes touchy. At a slip you can hose down the boat, make repairs, or hop to the shop for a bolt or a beer any time you feel like it; from a mooring the bother of getting ashore often persuades you not to go. But the mooring is cheaper and more readily available (at the Long Beach, Calif., marina, for example, the waiting list for one of its 2,000 slips is years long).

Slip rates range from $5 per foot of over-all boat length to about $20 per foot for a six- or seven-month season. A few of the lush, blue-blazer-class marinas, like Pier 66 in Fort Lauderdale, Fla., get 15 cents per foot per day! Moorings cost from about $60 to $300 for a season's use. For stowing the boat ashore, plan on spending one-quarter to one-half the in-the-water slip rate.

An alternative to using a marina is to join a yacht club (check your telephone directory); most clubs offer berthing facilities as one of their benefits. Generally these are moorings. And generally too few. Yacht club membership will stand you anywhere from $25 to $1,500 or so for the year—*if* the latter clubs will let you join. Besides berthing the boat if there is room, yacht club assets may include club restaurant, bar and golf links privileges, dinners, dances, organized racing, and the right to fly the club's burgee (flag).

Bills you can cut

Still left to consider are operating costs and the expense of repair. Operating costs are the factor over which you have most control. When the food bills are running high, simply buy more economical fare—frankfurters instead of steak. Or put everyone on a diet. When fuel bills spiral up, confine your cruising as necessary; you will discover also that cruising at moderate speeds burns less fuel than going all out, a point covered more fully in Chapter 4. And the cost of boat maintenance can be held to a minimum with a little initiative and ingenuity.

By initiative I mean gathering the energy to get off your transom and do what should be done on the boat before any real damage sets in from neglect; these steps are detailed in Chapter 13. By ingenuity I mean doing things in the best but cheapest way possible. For example, you will need a swab (mop) to swish down the deck at least at the end of the day. In a supermarket you can buy a mop for $1.90. The cheapest swab I find listed in a popular marine catalog sells for $3.95. There are many things you need aboard that are *uniquely* marine, items you will probably be unable to, and in any event should not, purchase anywhere except at a marine outlet. If the price of an item seems high, it may be because you are ignorant of its special qualities: heavy chroming, perhaps, to resist the highly corrosive effect of salt water; special gaskets to render the item waterproof; an airtight housing to make it vaporproof; and so on. Where safety is concerned, never substitute a shore-going version of some piece of equipment for the marine one, regardless of the difference in price. Where safety is not concerned, balance the cost of frequent replacement against the initial cost of buying the more durable item. But in a third category are items as suitable ashore as afloat, such as mops, plastic buckets, paintbrushes (but use only marine paint), sandpaper, masking tape, paperware, general detergents. These almost always are sold for less in a store serving the general public than in a marine shop. Hunt around and check before you buy.

If you are fairly faithful in your boat maintenance, you probably will have no major repair bills. By major I mean more than $100. To recondition a 10-inch-diameter aluminum propeller that has had a couple of seasons' ordinary use, you can expect to pay between $15 and $30, for example. A standby quart of topside (not for underwater use) marine paint will cost you between $5.50 and $7.20, a pint of varnish $1.90 to $3—both of which should be adequate for a season's touch-up work on any boat up to 25 feet. Unless you are lazy, sloppy, or plain unfortunate, the bulk of your repair work will consist of replacing screws and bolts that have worked free or were too small from the start. Always use a *marine* fastening, incidentally, to avoid rust and to get the strength necessary to cope with the stresses a small boat endures. The table of metals appropriate for boating uses shown on page 34 will help you to determine the kind of fastenings you will want to keep handy aboard.

Whatever fastening you choose, the cost of keeping a supply handy is negligible. A gross of 2″ No. 8 screws of high-quality silicon bronze alloy, for instance, will cost about $11. Cheap enough for the security it buys.

Okay, you're ready to pay

The sum you have reached if you have been tallying figures right along should be workably close—within a couple of hundred dollars—to what actual costs will be when you buy. What's more, you will have avoided buying a pig in a poke if you have followed the steps outlined in this chapter. Odds are your boat will be marvelously right in every way, and one you can afford. Or almost afford.

CHRYSLER
135

Chapter 3
WHAT'S FOR POWER?

Inboard engines, outboard motors, and inboard-outboard combinations ("stern-drives") are the forms of power plant in maximum marine use. Filling the fringes are jet-drives, rotary engines, air-drives, a few steam engines old and new, and here and there some totally oddball packages. One can generally expect to find boats powered this way: small boats, up to about 18 feet, will have outboards; medium-size boats, up to about 25 feet, inboard or stern-drive units; everything larger will be inboard-powered.

Outboards: from pill to prince

It is impossible to deny the outboard motor's place as a prime reason for the boating boom: of the nearly ten million pleasure boats on United States waters alone, more than half are outboard-powered. The outboard motor began as a small, portable, hand crank-started, handle-steered device that could be repaired quickly by carrying it from boat to shop. This trip, alas, was made too often. For a long time the outboard was a pill, a wheezy,

Thought to be the first mass-produced outboard motor, the 2-hp Waterman Porto was introduced in 1906.

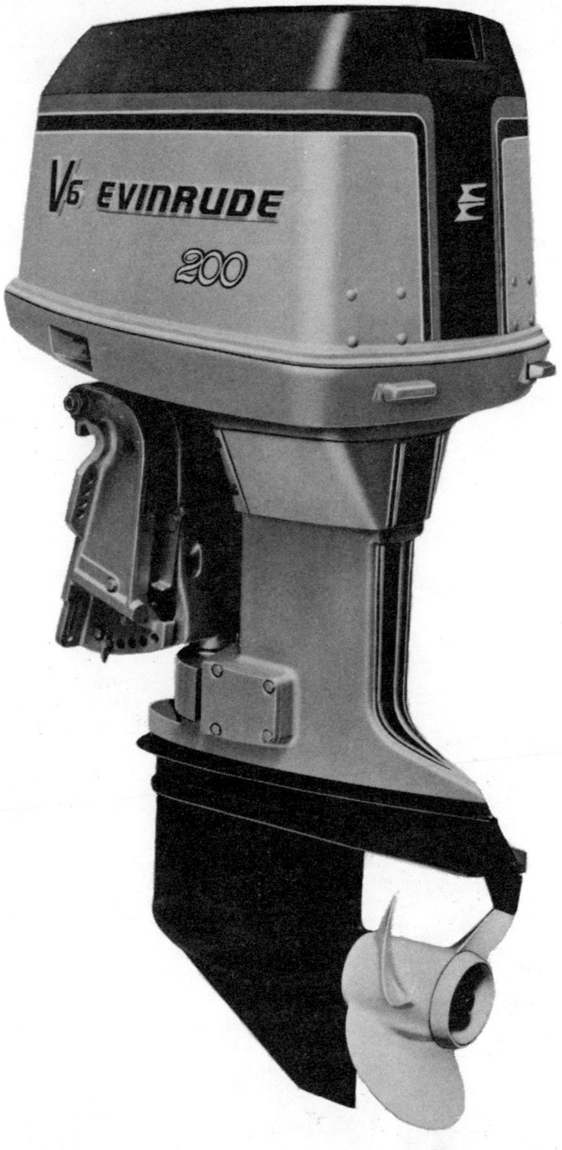

The 200-hp Evinrude, like the 200-hp Johnson, has 6 cylinders, built-in power tilt, and electric starting, and sells for about $3,000.

Volvo Penta has entered the outboard motor field with this 3-hp 30-pounder. It has built-in fuel tank and alternator.

smoky, cantankerous machine whose unpredictable refusals to start or run have inspired many a boatman to take up golf. It has grown into a prince. If hardly portable in the high-horsepower range—an 85 weighs about 270 pounds, a 200 some 380 pounds—it is nevertheless a delight to behold, a joy to operate, a remarkably dependable source of power that can be operated at wide-open speeds for as long as the fuel holds out. (A fuel-consumption rule-of-thumb, incidentally, is 1 gallon per hour for every 10 hp at open throttle.) When the modern outboard isn't working right, almost invariably it is fuel or spark afoul and the skipper's negligence rather than some motor defect at fault!

To the motor's bare beginnings have been added such technological assets as key starting, capacitor discharge ignition systems, single-lever remote control, effective silencing and tuned exhaust systems, solid-state alternators, stylish fiberglass and aluminum shrouds (covers), power motor tilts—the list is lengthy but the point is plain. Outboarding, which is powerboating's lower-budget end, has been given a goodly share of inboarding's pleasures.

Inside the outboard

With two exceptions all gasoline outboards are two-cycle affairs (one of every two piston strokes is a power stroke) and require oil to be mixed directly with the gasoline in ratios that vary with the make of the motor. (Apart from the scattering of electric trolling engines,

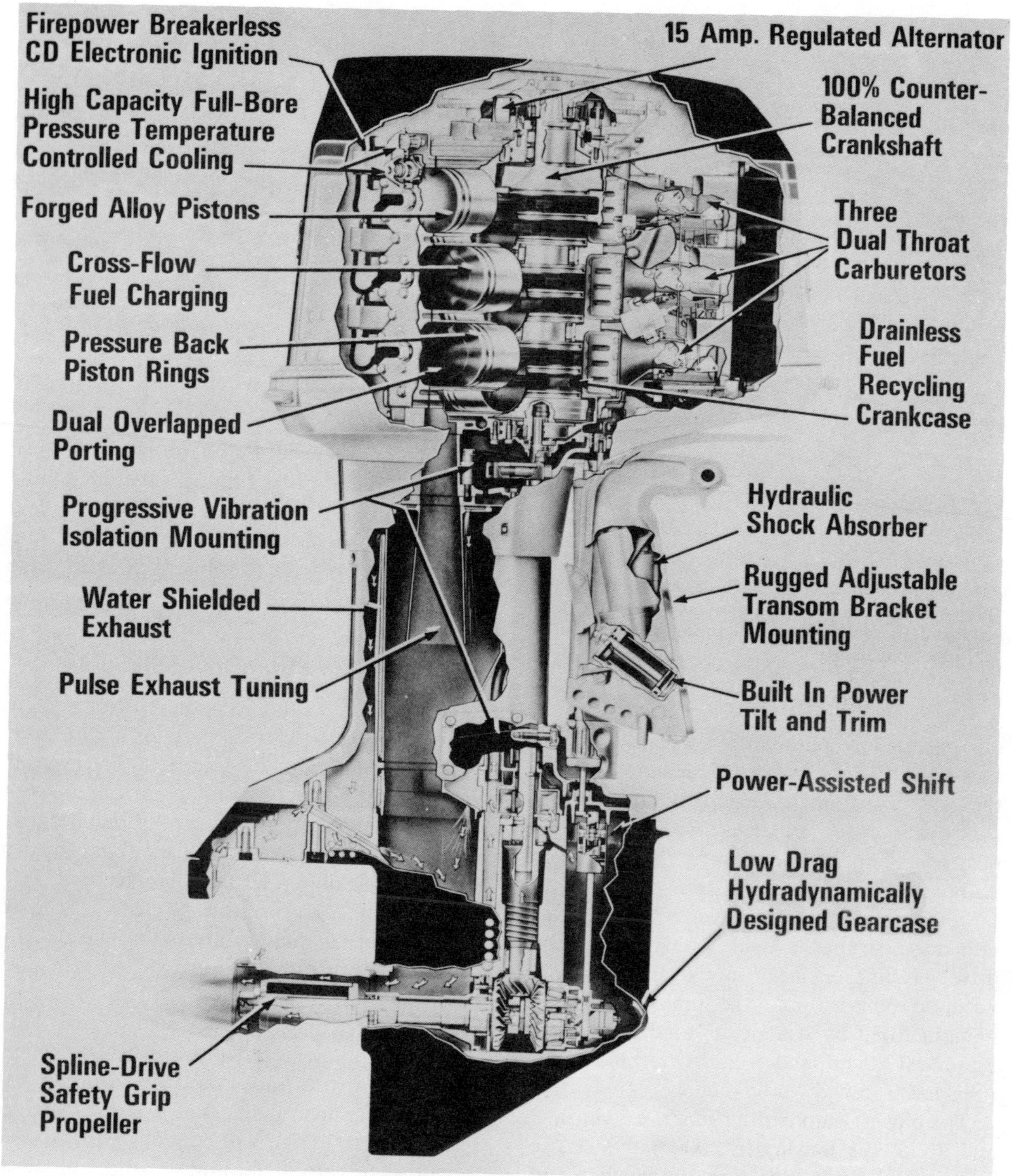

Anatomy of an outboard: Cutaway view is of Evinrude's V-6, 200-hp motor.

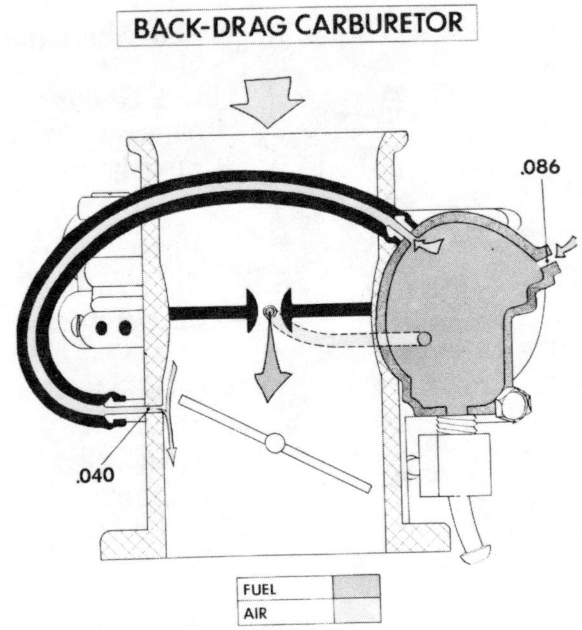

Since 1976 all Mercury outboards 40 hp and up have been equipped with "back drag" carburetors to help save fuel. Key is the air tube between the float bowl and the carb's side wall to control bowl pressure more efficiently.

Usual outboard is a single- or twin-motor setup. Here a professional racer worked out a triple threat, great on speed but a disaster on fuel.

all production outboards use gasoline for fuel.) When the mixture reaches the cylinders the gasoline vaporizes, leaving the oil to lubricate cylinder and crankcase walls and engine bearings. The exceptions are the four-cycle outboards (one of every four strokes is a power stroke), which have a separate oil crankcase, so that, as with inboard and stern-drive gasoline engines, only straight gasoline need be pumped into the tanks. These are manufactured by American Honda Motors in 7.5 and 17.5 hp models and Otterbine Industries in 2, 3, 5 and 7.5 hp models.

The biggest outboarding guns are Evinrude's and Johnson's 6-cylinder 200-hp models, introduced in 1976. It's hard to imagine outboards getting more powerful than that. (See "How Much for a Kicker?" on page 29 for the range of horsepower available in outboard motors.) More will require still heavier and larger engines, impractical and unsafe on conventionally designed outboard boats. I must confess, however, that I thought the same thing in the mid-'60s when Mercury led the field with its 110-hp package! The logical step from here, in any event, is to inboard or stern-drive power.

Getting the most from your outboard

All gasoline outboard motors are rated by their manufacturers for certain horsepower. You will be a rare bird indeed, however, if you get that horsepower in actual use, not because of any rating hanky-panky but because there are certain variables the boat owner should but seldom does take into account. Primarily these are trim and propeller. Trim is discussed in Chapter 5, and so we need concern ourselves only with propeller selection here.

Almost any marine dealer who services outboard motors will have test wheels (called "paddles" in the trade) and an accurate tachometer (an instrument that measures engine rpm). With these he will conduct a two-phase test, the first to determine if the outboard motor is in fact capable of producing its rated horsepower, and the other to determine if the motor will do so with a given propeller under the "load" conditions to which you will put the boat.

First he will clamp the motor in a test tank (often a battered garbage can filled with water) or at a dockside testing installation and with the tachometer note the engine's rpm reading with a test wheel. It should come up to the manufacturer's minimum rpm range specification, usually noted in the owner's motor manual. If it does not, which is rare, something is wrong with the motor. If it does the dealer is ready for phase two.

The boat is loaded with as much weight as will generally be aboard, and the motor is clamped astern. The propeller installed for this first load trial can be chosen from any one of a dozen propeller selection charts that propeller manufacturers, among others, publish or, as is more often the case, from the dealer's notion of what the right propeller should be. In either case it is only a starting point. With this propeller in place and the tachometer hooked up, the boat is run at full throttle and the rpm reading is weighed against the recommended specification. If the rpm fails to reach the proper range, the propeller pitch (angle of the blades) is probably too great. Continue to operate the boat this way and the motor will be overloaded, causing anything from pre-ignition (which ruins pistons and spark plugs) to poor acceleration. If the rpm exceeds the recommended range, more pitch is needed. Allowing an engine to turn up too high for extended periods plays havoc with the powerhead.

You needn't spend much time on the question of blade number. A two-bladed prop is best for racing, a four-blader for smooth cruising at reduced rpm, and a three-blader the most practical compromise. That's why the three-blader is standard on most new boats.

Stainless steel is the most durable prop material but also the most expensive, with bronze hard on its heels. Aluminum, however, remains the most popular for outboards, I suppose because it's cheaper. Various plastics keep popping up as the principal prop material but as yet haven't taken hold. One manufacturer of propellers who has been pushing plastic implies that because plastic props change shape under high rpm this is an asset. It isn't. The change occurs in the wrong direction: the blades tend to flatten.

A few trial runs with various propellers will uncover the model that is just right for your boat and the use to which you will put it.

The right size of propeller can make a whopping difference in the performance you get from your boating rig. Take the time to find out which prop is best for you.

A modern melding: the stern-drive

Not until 1961 did the stern-drive appear on the marine scene in quantity (the gasoline inboard already held sway in 1910), but there is little doubt that it has come to stay. The stern-drive is a blend of inboard and outboard concepts, aimed at holding the former's advantages of reliability, ample torque, and relatively low fuel consumption and the latter's tiltability and minimal underwater drag. It consists mainly of an inboard engine placed all the way aft and coupled through the transom

A blend of inboard power and outboard drive, the stern-drive has taken a major portion of the marine propulsion market. Model here is 165-hp Mer-Cruiser.

to an outboard-type drive unit, called an outdrive.

Generally the outdrive can be tilted, allowing the boat to be beached easily or operated in shoal waters; the drive can also be cranked completely free of the water, so that someone aboard can clear a fouled propeller or replace a battered one. Also, so possible corrosion can be avoided when the boat is left for a few days or more. The design provides a certain degree of portability, too, in that the outdrive can be detached and carried to the shop for repair. If the inboard engine portion is ailing, however, the problem is identical to that of the pure inboard's: the work will have to be done aboard or the engine or boat may have to be hauled.

When pondering the advisability of buying a stern-drive boat or installing a stern-drive in the boat you already own, consider the boat's design. Can it safely accommodate the weight aft or will it perilously or uneconomically drag its rump? On new boats, this factor probably has been considered, though it will not hurt to get the opinion of a disinterested boat designer. Be sure to do this for any boat initially designed for anything other than stern-drive propulsion.

The following table indicates price range of gasoline stern-drive packages from which you can choose.

A Sampling of Stern-Drives

Make	*Horsepower*	*Weight*	*Price*
Stokes Marine	120	390	$2,935
Stokes Marine	120*	1,025	5,635
OMC	140	618	2,600
Holman Moody	215	791	3,500
OMC	235	862	3,335
Holman Moody	380	685	5,700

* Diesel; all others listed here use gasoline.

Boating's big daddy: the inboard

In essential respects the gasoline-fed inboard engine is similar to the ordinary automobile engine, but modified or manufactured to do a somewhat different job in a wholly different environment. For cooling, the inboard commonly draws upon the surrounding fresh or salt water instead of utilizing a closed, recirculating system as is done in a car. (There are closed, fresh-water cooling systems available for boats.) As with all other forms of marine propulsion, the inboard has only one "forward" gear; it also has a neutral position and a reverse gear, the latter comprising the powerboat's only effective "braking" mechanism.

Inboards have changed drastically from slow-speed, low-rpm products to more muscular machines, calling on high compression and rpm, reduction gears (devices which reduce revolutions in the transmission of power from engine to propeller, allowing the latter to turn at a more efficient rate), modern metals, and high-octane fuel for sustenance, longevity, and output.

The inboard's horsepower range for pleasure boats starts with auxiliary needs at 7.5 horsepower or so and slides up to about 580 for big boats that need it and, to the dismay of Coast Guardsmen and conservationists,

Osco 4550L, a 320-hp V-8 gasoline inboard.

Westerbeke model Six-346 diesel inboard turns up 115 horsepower, has 2:1 hydraulic transmission, and is fresh-water cooled.

smaller ones that do not. It is possible to categorize inboards as heavy-duty, medium-duty, and high-speed, but it would be meaningless to bracket these by horsepower range, because it is the *ratio* of power to hull form, size, and weight that controls.

The following table indicates the range of gasoline inboard engines from which you can choose.

The inboard engines—gasoline

Make	*Horsepower*	*Weight*	*Price*
Stokes Marine	7.5	89 lbs.	$ 850
Holman Moody	215	617	1,795
Hardin	240	693	2,000
OMC	260	824	3,000
Stokes	330	850	2,150
Holman Moody	340	870	2,900
Holman Moody	580	865	7,000

Distinguishing the two

One further consideration deserves attention here, the choice between gasoline and diesel engines.

Both types are internal combustion engines: one way or another they get air and fuel into the cylinders and ignite the mixture. Compression makes the difference. In the gasoline engine a carburetor-blended mixture of gasoline and air is drawn into the cylinders, compressed by pistons, and ignited by an electric spark produced by the spark plug. Into the diesel's cylinder mere air is drawn (and so a carburetor is unnecessary) and compressed to a much greater degree with a resultant higher temperature than occurs in the gasoline engine. Diesel fuel is then injected into the cylinder where it is ignited and vaporized spontaneously by the heat, eliminating any need for spark plugs.

All stock outboard motors and most inboard engines are fueled by gasoline. Inasmuch as the diesel has fewer parts and operates on somewhat less costly fuel, why hasn't it booted gasoline right off the market? Engine weight, size, and initial cost are why. To withstand the greater pressure that the diesel's high compression produces, its parts must be heavier than those of a corresponding gasoline engine—and hence costlier (compare tables on pages 45 and 46). The greater initial expense, it is true, may be compensated for in fuel-cost savings if the boat is used long and frequently enough, but the diesel's weight and size remain critical factors for most pleasure boats. This explains why the diesel receives its warmest reception on commercial fishing boats and on motor yachts where weight, size, and initial cost are borne easily. Continual manufacturing progress, however, is reducing the diesel's weight, size, and cost aspects to reach a greater marine market.

The following table indicates the range of diesel inboard engines from which you can choose.

The inboard engines—diesel

Make	*Horsepower*	*Weight*	*Price*
Petter	6½	210 lbs.	$1,899
Perkins	50	490	3,000
Holman Moody	52	630	4,000
Farymann	68	950	5,150
Starboard	75	747	3,290
Stokes	80	825	3,300
Johnson & Towers	101	1,180	4,000
Perkins	130	1,132	5,200

How many horses?

Any given hull can be efficiently driven just so quickly and no more, regardless of how much more power is applied. Excessive power will exact a toll in wasted fuel, poor boat performance, decreased safety—or all these together. But how much is too much?

The answer is easily ascertained for outboard boats (other than inflatables) less than 20 feet long and built since November 1972. They must display a capacity plate—officially it's known as a "U. S. Coast Guard Capacity Information Label"—which lists the maximum horsepower the hull can handle safely.

Anatomy of a diesel: Cutaway view is of Perkins 4-cylinder, 50-hp model.

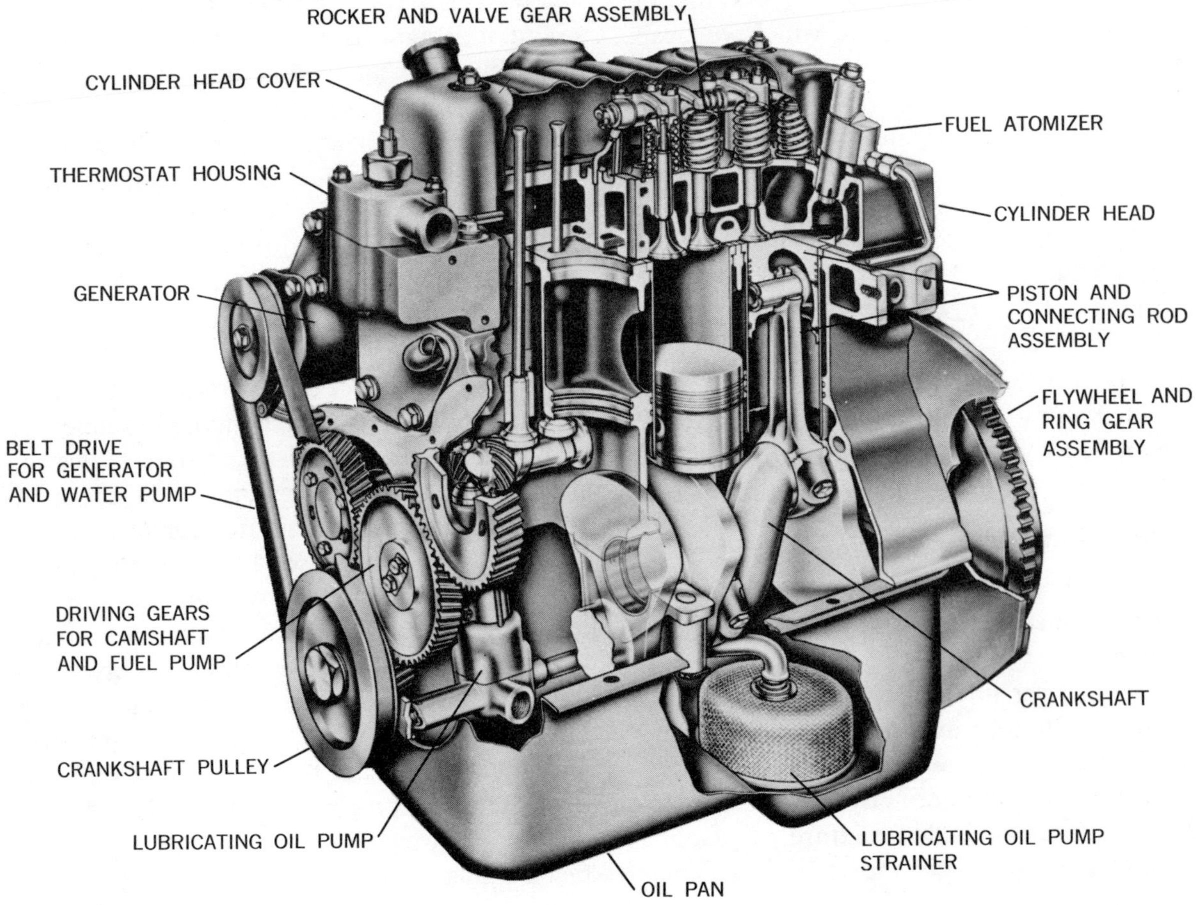

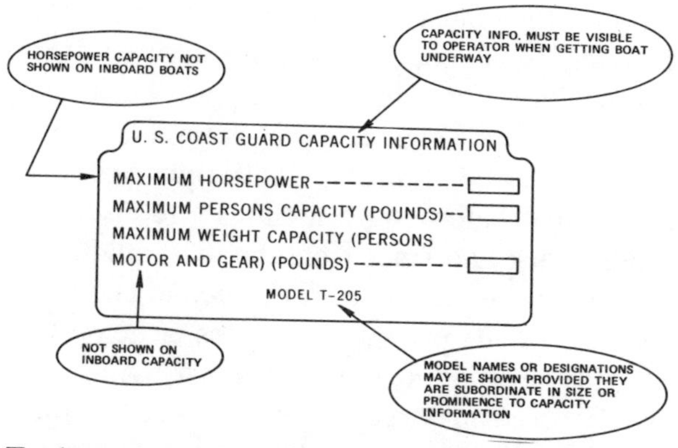

To determine horsepower capacity of outboard boats less than 20 feet long, look for the metal capacity plate that must be displayed in the hull somewhere near the helm.

Before you buy the outboard motor, get the dealer to let you try that model on your boat. Dealers have demonstrator motors for this purpose. If ordinary observation indicates a mismatch of boat and power, you at least have a starting point from which to estimate how many "horses" you can safely use.

Do not hesitate, incidentally, to write to the boatbuilder for his recommendation of maximum safe horsepower if it is not provided with the boat. He has probably tested the boat with every outboard motor that might do the job. When writing, tell him how many people and what gear you generally will have aboard.

Inboarders must ask

Purchasers of inboard boats, and these include stern-drive models, and outboards 20 feet and longer do not have it as easy. No simple formula has been developed for the layman by which a safe horsepower-to-boat ratio can be discovered. The reason most often advanced for this lack is that hull variables on inboard boats (especially design, over-all weight, and weight distribution) are too great. If, as is frequently the case, you have some choice of how much horsepower will be installed in your new boat, or if you plan to repower an old boat, the following three suggestions may be helpful: (1) ask a marine surveyor (see page 31); or (2) ask a naval architect (check the Yellow Pages or write to the Society of Naval Architects & Marine Engineers, 74 Trinity Place, New York, N.Y. 10006); or (3) ask the boatbuilder.

The surveyor and the architect, unless they know the boat in question, will want to see it before suggesting appropriate horsepower. You can keep their fee nominal, however, by supplying a blueprint or line drawing of the hull, either of which you should be able to get from the builder. Inform them (or the builder, if he is your choice): (1) what approximate speed you want from the boat; (2) to what use you will put it most of the time (cruising? skiing? fishing? etc.); (3) in what waters you will operate; and (4) approximately how many persons will usually be aboard.

The options offered

To illustrate the horsepower spread available for particular inboard boats (all gasoline-powered models) consider this baker's dozen of 1976 listings.

Boat	*Hp Option*
16′7″ Century runabout	233 hp to 250 hp
18′ Correct Craft runabout	225 hp to 330 hp
21′ Penn Yan runabout	225 hp to 260 hp
24′ Trojan cruiser	225 hp to 233 hp
25′ Luhrs skiff	225 hp to 250 hp
25′10″ Pacemaker cruiser	220 hp to 270 hp
26′8″ Tollycraft cruiser	255 hp to twin 165 hp
27½′ Omega cruiser	twin 220 hp to twin 300 hp
28′ Silverton cruiser	225 hp to 250 hp
30′7″ Bertram cruiser	twin 225 hp to twin 350 hp
32′ Forest Johnson cruiser	twin 160 hp to twin 225 hp

One engine or two? Generally it's a question of what you can afford. There's greater safety, but also expense, with two; there's less weight and so more speed, as on this bass boat, with a single motor astern.

Boat	*Hp Option*
36′ Hatteras cruiser	twin 330 hp to twin 203† hp
41′ Chris-Craft cruiser	twin 330 hp to twin 286† hp

† Diesel

One engine or two?

Except for small motors—say up to 20 horsepower—the most compelling argument for deriving your boat's propulsive power from two engines (these are "twin-screw" boats) instead of one ("single-screw") is safety. Should one engine fail, the other will chug you into port. Small motors presumably are used on small boats, and since small boats should stick close to shore their need for a second engine is lessened by the probable nearness of help. The most devastating argument against twin-screw installations on larger boats is price: it may cost from a little more to a whale of a lot more, depending on engine make, difficulty of installation, and the elaborateness of the fuel system necessary. Sometimes the additional weight of two engines rather than one prohibits a twin-screw installation.

If boat and budget can stand the two-engine setup, however, choose it by all means—for safety primarily, as has been said, but also for the ease of boat handling it provides, particularly on inboard boats. One major reason for this is that the two propellers are located toward the sides of the bottom of the boat rather than, as is the case with a single engine, amidships (in the center). Merely putting either of two engines into "forward" or "reverse" causes an immediate turning effect. Moreover, the twin-screw boat can be swung in pretty much its own length by simultaneously putting one engine into "forward" and the other into "reverse." This makes docking, nemesis of the new boatman, a simple maneuver, capable of being mastered after very few tries.

Chapter 4
THE FUEL SYSTEM

All the precautions necessary for the safe construction and installation of your boat's permanent fuel system will already have been taken by the builder—well, by most builders. You should check by comparing the system with standards recommended by the National Fire Protection Association, 60 Batterymarch St., Boston, Mass. 02110. Its 56-page booklet (ask for NFPA 302, *Motor Craft;* $1) is invaluable too when you want to replace or install new fuel tanks or fuel fittings. The rest—inspection and maintenance of the system (see Chapter 13) and the following checklist of safe fueling procedures—is in your care. Your aim throughout is to prevent fuel leaks and eliminate sources of gasoline or diesel vapor ignition. Here's how:

Like this model by Cole-Hersee, switches for a boat's electrical system should be designed for marine use: vaporproof, waterproof, and rustproof.

Checklist of fueling procedures

Before fueling:

☐ Douse all lighted cigarettes, cigars, and pipes, and alert passengers and anyone else nearby to avoid smoking.

☐ Switch off, preferably with a vaporproof, marine-type main switch, all equipment capable of producing a spark or flame.

☐ Close all doors, ports, hatches, and windows.

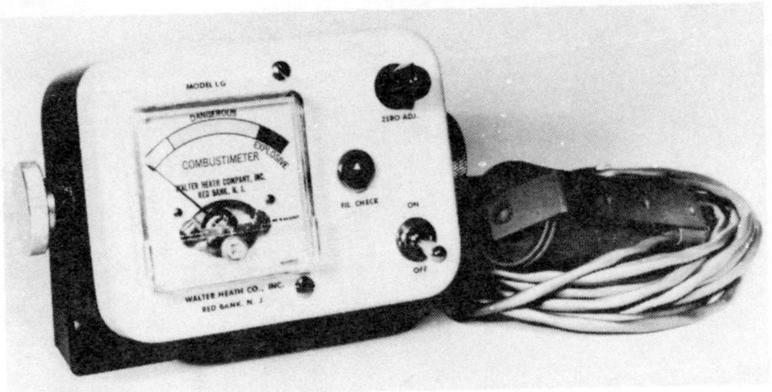

Used with discretion, which means you should not rely solely on it, a fume detector, or "sniffer," warns of dangerous buildups in the bilges.

- ☐ Recheck the boat's lines and fenders ("bumpers") for security at the gas dock.
- ☐ See that a filled fire extinguisher is nearby.

While fueling:

- ☐ Remind everyone not to smoke.
- ☐ By making metal-to-metal contact, ground the gas pump nozzle against the fill pipe to avoid static sparks. The entire fuel system, of course, as NFPA standards explain in detail, should be grounded.
- ☐ Guard against spilling or sloshing fuel aboard. Estimating how much fuel you need will help to nip overflow.

After fueling:

- ☐ Announce that everyone can smoke soon, but not yet.
- ☐ Wipe up or hose down any fuel spillage on the boat.
- ☐ Dispose of oily or fuel-soaked rags ashore.
- ☐ Open the boat for ventilation.
- ☐ Sniff for fumes. If clear, run blowers.
- ☐ Do not under any circumstances start the engine until all fuel vapors are gone.
- ☐ Execute a regular program of fuel-system inspection and maintenance. What you especially want to keep tabs on are the condition and security of the following:
  - the tanks and their supports;
  - the fuel pipes and tubings and their connections; and
  - the fuel strainers and filters.

A bilge blower is an effective item of safety equipment, helping to clear the boat of potentially explosive fumes.

Closing the airways

No other fueling precaution is as slippery to grasp in concept as that which calls for the closing of all doors, ports, hatches, and windows before fueling. One's natural inclination is to open everything to provide ventilation. The catch is that openings permit fumes to permeate the boat and, because they are heavier than air, sink to the lowest parts, where removal is difficult. Close up and keep closed until you have finished fueling. Even when you fill portable tanks on the pier or gas dock, which is where they should be filled if they are still portable when full, the boat should be closed to keep out wind-borne vapors.

Once you are through fueling, open all the airways you have closed, the doors, ports, etc., so that what wind there is will sweep through the boat, helping to whisk away lingering fumes. Bilge blowers, if you have them, should be turned on only *after* you have sniffed the bilge to detect fumes. A bilge blower is a sealed (no sparks) electronic device that sucks in air at one end and discharges it overboard at the other. It gets rid of fumes but will not alert you to their presence. That is why *you* should check first—open the hatch, poke

If you're trailering your boat or if you need only a few gallons of fuel, there's no reason why you shouldn't buy the fuel at any service station ashore. Under all other circumstances, however, fuel up at a gas dock: one gallon of gas weighs slightly more than 6 pounds. (*Photo by the author.*)

your face in, and sniff; the odor is unmistakable. If fumes are present it behooves you to learn why: leaky tank? defective coupling? cracked hose? Then correct the condition immediately. If your nose indicates all's well, run the blowers for a few minutes anyhow. Then close whatever vents you want to, pay the man, and go. Oh yes, you can smoke now.

Most probable defects

The following list gives fuel system defects which the standards already referred to would eliminate. They are highlighted here, however, because they are the most common culprits.

- ☐ Inadequate tank material, either because of insufficient strength or corrosion resistance.
- ☐ Inaccessibility of fuel tank (for inspection) or fuel line shut-off valve.
- ☐ No marine-type shut-off valve at tank end, engine end, or both.
- ☐ Improper grounding of fuel system.
- ☐ Fuel tank vent-overflow pipe is too small and is unscreened at discharge end.
- ☐ Insufficient ventilation of fuel tank and engine areas.
- ☐ Incorrect type of fittings used.

Where to buy your fuel

There is no inherent difference between the gasoline sold at marinas for boats and the gasoline sold at service stations for cars. This observation raises the question of why the marina's price might be a nickel or so more per gallon. Probably the higher price reflects the seasonal nature of the boating business in many parts of the Northern Hemisphere and, in some instances, the difficulty of trucking fuel to the marina site. If you are faced with such a price differential and need only a small supply of fuel for the day, there is no reason why you should not buy it ashore and bring it to the boat (use a portable fuel container to transport it). But if you must handle more than three or four gallons, pay the marina the extra nickel and keep your intestines intact. Gasoline weighs a bit over six pounds per gallon.

(*Photo by the author.*)

Chapter 5
TRIM: HOW MANY PEOPLE?

People are mobile, whether ashore or afloat. They walk around, climb on top of, duck beneath, hang over, sprawl forward, congregate aft, slip, slide, run, jump, and choose the worst possible moments to visit the head. Because their number and distribution aboard critically affect the performance and safety of the boat, you, as skipper, must regulate these factors—for which you'll be less loved.

Parts of the improper boat-load problem are easily handled: restrict your invitations to avoid overloading, and install or stow equipment to help provide optimum boat trim (balance). Boat stability is what you seek. Designers can calculate stability to a neat fraction for a given boat with a given weight, but their arithmetic presupposes fixed factors, and people are seldom fixed, in this sense of the word. Still, a known limitation on people and pounds is a guideline, and boatbuilders now are required to provide it on certain models.

The capacity plate

In the United States, the Coast Guard, Boating Safety Advisory Council, and various boating organizations have co-operated in developing a uniform maximum person/pounds standard for boatbuilders who since 1972 have been required to affix this information to certain boats in the form of a "boat capacity plate." The limitation is given in both persons and pounds so that the skipper can adjust for the young or rotund. It appears likely that eventually every boat sold in this country will display a capacity plate.

If your boat does not have one, the dealer or boatbuilder or a surveyor should be able to furnish a recommendation. In any event a look at your boat in action will inform you of improper load. Such actual observation is much preferred over the unreliable saw of having 12 cubic feet of space for each 150-pound passenger. Begin by dispersing equipment and gear evenly (by weight) throughout the boat. Passengers, ideally, should be distributed and kept the same way. How much you need compromise with this ideal depends on the dimensions of the boat (the larger and weightier, the less effect added

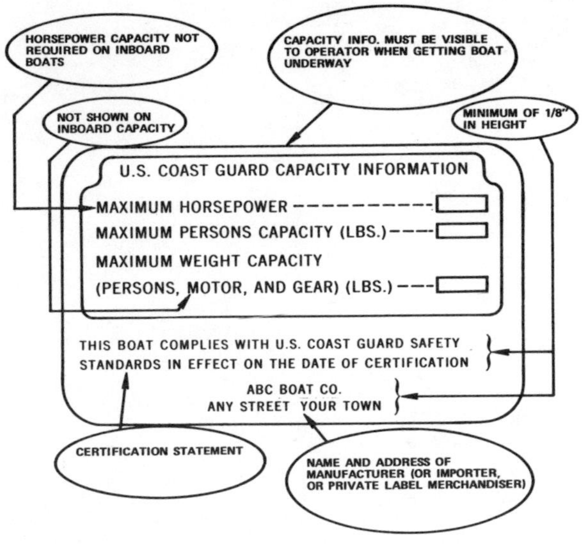

Certain boats must display a metal capacity plate that tells how much weight the boat can handle. The plate here is combined with a builder's "statement of compliance" with Coast Guard standards in effect at the time (see non-combined capacity plate on page 53).

1. Apart from the fact that the boat is illegally overloaded with people, note how the concentration of weight forward is burying the bow, making steering perilously difficult.

poundage will have) and the prevailing water conditions (the nastier the seas, the stricter the requirements for safe trim). Now observe what is happening to the boat, and adjust the position and the quantity of gear or people as necessary. You want to avoid two things: taking on "solid water" (as opposed to spray, for example), which may swamp or capsize the boat; and radically trimming by the stern (squatting) or bow (digging or burying), which will hamper maneuverability.

Bow riders and side sitters

Sitting on the bow and on the boat's covering boards ("side decks") are perpetual problems. Everyone loves to do it. It is obvious that such extreme placement of weight may trim a small boat badly. More pressingly, you may lose a guest or two if the boat lurches in some unanticipated direction, shoved perhaps by a maverick sea or swung deliberately to avoid debris. Side-sitting, I suggest, should be flatly prohibited. Bow-riding need not be (except in certain states such as New Hampshire where, like side-sitting, it is unlawful), and the delights of being bathed in spray and scrubbed by wind argue for permitting it. Use your discretion, taking into account trim, water conditions (anything other than "calm" is probably unsafe), and the probable maturity of the sitters (kids are not necessarily immature; if permitted on the bow they should be made to wear life preservers, however). Always keep an eye on your bow riders, holding the boat speed down and never permitting your forward visibility to be impaired.

Another boat-loading abuse, growing in seriousness, is the carrying of excessive weight too high. This, technically, raises the vessel's intended center of gravity. The practical result is that the boat may roll more deeply than it should, increasing its likelihood of capsizing. Occasionally, the builder himself is responsible, adding a flying bridge, for instance, on a boat that has not been designed for it. More often it is the fault of the boatman who permits too many people on the bridge or deckhouse top.

As skipper you're liable

It does not take an experienced hand to discern improper load. There is another compelling reason why you should. Besides existing statutory law both in the United States and in Canada making negligent boat operation a crime punishable by fine or imprisonment, a civil suit may be in the offing. By virtue of being skipper you become bound to exercise such skill and knowledge as would be used by the "ordinary, prudent and reasonable" skipper in similar circumstances—the standard of conduct applied in trials involving negligence. This alone seems sufficient inducement to learn the fundamentals of safe boating, to train yourself to respond intelligently to foreseeable situations, and to carry adequate personal liability insurance.

The skill required, I hasten to add, is not formidable; it is grounded in common sense, no more, which helps to explain why so many people in all parts of the free world are turning for their pleasures to the nearest available boating waters, and why boating continues to be among the safest participating sports available.

2. Congregating aft doesn't help matters, because now the boat is squatting severely, reducing the helmsman's forward visibility and the boat's stability.

3. Avoid overloading and, by distributing the weight evenly, eliminate improper trim and the boat will perform as she was designed to: safely.

Know what's missing? Registration numbers, for one thing, and proper personal flotation devices (PFDs). All recreational boats must carry at least one approved PFD for each person aboard. If the boat is 16 feet or longer, as here, the minimum PFDs must be of Types I, II, or III; the four cushions shown are Type IV PFDs.

Chapter 6
EQUIPPING THE BOAT—I

Certain boating equipment is prescribed by law—federal, state, or both. Because all "navigable" waterways of the United States—coastal portions of the Atlantic and Pacific oceans, the Mississippi and Potomac rivers, the Great Lakes are examples—are under the jurisdiction of the federal government, boats operating on them are subject to federal regulation. There is no easy way to learn which waters are navigable ones. That they are tidal, for example, the test in England, does not control in the United States. One key is whether or not the water is "navigable in fact" for international or interstate public travel or trade. If in doubt about the character of the waters you will use, ask the local Coast Guard office or write to the U. S. Coast Guard, Office of Boating Safety, Washington, D.C. 20590.

On "non-navigable" waters—California's Salton Sea, the North Platte River in Nebraska and Wyoming, New Jersey's Lake Hopatcong are examples—you must look to local authority, usually the state, to determine what *must* be aboard.

On navigable waters the basic legislation regulating equipment continues to be the Motorboat Act of 1940 plus such regulations as may be implemented from time to time by the Department of Transportation (or whatever department the Coast Guard happens to be included under at the time) under the Federal Boat Safety Act of 1971. On some navigable waters a state may have a concurrent right to specify equipment so long as it does not conflict with or in any way diminish federal standards. The state sometimes requires more. Sources for state information appear on page 104; for federal information, on page 106.

First, find your class

Certain equipment requirements under federal law vary with the class of powerboat you have. Class is based on boat length. This is found by measuring the hull proper in a straight, level line from end to end over the deck or where the deck would be if the boat had one. The classes are:

Class A: less than 16 feet.

Class 1: 16 feet to less than 26 feet.

Minimum required powerboat equipment on U.S. waters

Equipment	*Class A*	*Class 1*	*Class 2*	*Class 3*
Backfire flame arrestor	One approved[1] device on each carburetor of gasoline engines installed after April 25, 1940; not required on outboard motors.			
Ventilators	At least two ducted ventilators fitted with cowls or equivalent to sufficiently ventilate the spaces of every engine and fuel-tank compartment of boats constructed or decked over after April 25, 1940 and using gasoline or other fuel of a flashpoint under 110° F.			
Bell	None[2]	None[2]	One which when struck produces a "clear, bell-like tone of full rounded characteristics."	
Personal Flotation Devices	One Type I, II, III, or IV for each person.	One Type I, II, or III for each person on board or being towed on water skiis, etc., plus one Type IV available to be thrown.		
Whistle	None[2]	One hand-, mouth-, or power-operated, audible for at least ½ mile	One hand- or power-operated, audible for at least 1 mile.	One power-operated, audible for at least 1 mile
Fire extinguisher[3]—portable. When no fixed fire extinguishing system is installed in machinery space(s)	At least one B-I type-approved hand portable extinguisher. None required on open outboards smaller than 26 feet		At least two B-I type-approved hand portable extinguishers; or at least one B-II type-approved hand portable extinguisher	At least three B-I type-approved hand portable extinguishers; or at least one B-I type plus one B-II type-approved hand portable extinguisher
When fixed fire extinguishing system is installed in machinery space(s)	None	None	At least one B-I type-approved hand portable extinguisher	At least two B-I type-approved hand portable extinguishers; or at least one B-II type-approved hand portable extinguisher
Sanitation devices	On all boats having installed toilet facilities; see text for detailed explanation.			

[1] "Approved" with respect to required equipment means approved by the Coast Guard; brand names are given in CG-190, "Equipment Lists," available free from any Coast Guard Marine Inspection Office.

[2] Although the Motorboat Act of 1940 does not specify this equipment for these classes, "Rules of the Road" (see pages 81ff.) do not excuse any class from having to sound the proper signals.

[3] B-1 extinguishers contain: 1¼ to 2½ gallons foam; or 4 to 15 pounds carbon dioxide; or 2 to 10 pounds dry chemical; or 2½ pounds freon. The B-II extinguishers contain: 2½ gallons foam; or 15 pounds carbon dioxide; or 10 to 20 pounds dry chemical.

Class 2: 26 feet to less than 40 feet.
Class 3: 40 feet to 65 feet.

Now, with your class known and your state control checked out, you will find out on the facing page what federal laws call for.

Essential equipment in Canada

In Canada the Small Vessel Regulations establish the minimum powerboat equipment, including lights, required by the government. A copy is available from the Queen's Printer, Ottawa. A handy condensation of these regulations is distributed free by the Department of Transport, Marine Regulations Branch, Ottawa (ask for the booklet *Safety Afloat*). A United States boat properly equipped under United States law need not comply with Canadian equipment regulations if it is cruising Canadian waters temporarily. Similarly, Canadian craft visiting United States waters are exempted from United States equipment regulations.

For cleaner waters

It is often said that the term "head" came into use for the marine toilet because in square-rigger days the crew went to the bow, or head, of the boat, hung from the bowsprit or figurehead in a rope rigging, and did their biological thing. Thus one went to the head.

Whatever the truth, marine heads have received considerable attention in the United States ever since the Environmental Protection Agency set out standards for what could and could not be discharged into our waters. These standards, which have been implemented by the Coast Guard, require that on fresh-water lakes, reservoirs, and other fresh-water impoundments "whose inlets or outlets are such as to prevent the ingress or egress by vessel traffic"—meaning essentially landlocked bodies of fresh water—and on rivers not capable of interstate navigation, *all* discharge of sewage and waste is prohibited. To be legal on such waters your boat must either not have a head or have the head so secured as to be incapable of discharging overboard.

Waters on which a Coast Guard-certified marine sanitation device—MSD is what it is called—which permits discharge are allowed to include all coastal waters, the Great Lakes and their interconnected waterways, and "other flowing waters that are navigable interstate . . ."

What type of MSD should your boat have? If you regularly boat on waters in which no discharge, treated or untreated, is permitted, you'll want to consider a holding tank, which is a Type III MSD. You'll want to consider it, that is, provided there are sites bordering the waterways you use with pump-out facilities for the holding tank. Increasingly these are being installed by marinas and by municipalities.

A Type I MSD means that its effluent, or discharge, has no visible floating solids and an E. coliform bacteria count not greater than 1,000 per 100 milliliters.

A Type II MSD means that the bacterial count is not greater than 200 per 100 milliliters and that suspended solids do not exceed 150 milligrams per liter.

I don't exactly appreciate what all those figures mean either. It is more important that you know whether you need a Type I, II, or III MSD, and the table on the next page tells you.

The right lights

Powerboats on United States waters, while under way or while anchored outside federal anchorage areas, must display certain lights between sunset and sunrise "and during such time no other lights which may be mistaken for those prescribed shall be exhibited . . ." A powerboat is under way when it is not at anchor, not made fast to the shore, and not aground. Away from the high seas, the skipper may light his vessel according to Inland or International Rules. The high seas are those waters beyond a designated offshore line, and *only* International running lights may be used there.

Vessel type	Must be equipped with a	Unless equipped with
Existing—a vessel whose construction was initiated before January 30, 1975.	Coast Guard-certified Type II or Type III MSD after January 30, 1980.	On or before January 30, 1978, with any USCG-certified flow-through device, which may be used for its operable life. A USCG-certified Type I device installed after January 30, 1978, must be replaced by January 31, 1980, with a USCG-certified Type II or Type III device.
New—a vessel whose construction was initiated on or after January 30, 1975.	Coast Guard-certified Type I, Type II, or Type III MSD on and after January 30, 1977.	
	Coast Guard-certified Type II or Type III MSD after January 30, 1980.	A Coast Guard-certified Type I MSD installed on or before January 30, 1980, which may be used for the operable life of the device.

Lights are required to be visible for a given arc when viewed from certain directions. Mariners express this arc in points, each point being equal to 11¼ degrees. Now we have a handy reference. For example, if we want to call our buddy's attention to some bikini-draped boat going by 22½ degrees off the starboard bow more or less, we need only direct him to *"two points* off the starboard bow." With limits, a 32-point light is one visible from all-around, or 360°; a 10-point light, one visible for 112°; and so on. Later, when we discuss right of way, you will see this system used again. If night running is on your agenda, the lights you'll need are shown on page 62.

At anchor

Boats less than 150 feet long, which covers every one I know, must carry an anchor light when swinging on the hook for the night. This white, 32-point light must be placed "forward, where it can best be seen" for at least 2 miles. On the Great Lakes, the light must be set no more than 20 feet above the hull and be visible for a minimum of only one mile. "Visibility" throughout these lighting requirements means visibility on a dark, clear night.

Motorboats smaller than 65 feet and anchored in special anchorage areas are not required to show an anchor light. The Army (Corps of Engineers) designates these anchorage grounds; the Department of Transportation (Coast Guard) marks them; and the Defense Mapping Agency Hydrographic Center charts them. Since the law does not *prohibit* the use of an anchor light in these areas, I always burn one if I'm aboard. Its purpose is to alert others to the presence of an anchored boat; skippers are presumed to know of the presence of an anchored boat when they enter an anchorage area, but maybe they don't.

On the high seas, International Rules call for a 2-mile, 32-point white anchor light.

Free "Rules of the Road" booklets are yours for the asking. Write to Commandant, U. S. Coast Guard Headquarters, Washington, D.C. 20226. Specify which you want: CG-169, Inland and International Rules; CG-172, Great Lakes Rules; or CG-184, Western Rivers Rules.

Running lights—but what for?

The system of lights I have been talking about informs the nighttime observer that (1) a boat is there; (2) it is about so many feet long; and (3) it is anchored or heading in a given direction—all of which information might otherwise be lost in the dark. With practice the observer can tell also how fast the vessel is moving. Item (3), learning what the boat is doing by the lights one sees, needs explanation.

Sidelights and combination lights *always* show red on the boat's port (left, facing forward) side and green on its starboard. Each light is rigged to cast a beam over an unbroken 10-point arc from dead ahead to two points abaft (behind) the beam. Stern lights, anchor lights, and single (i.e., not combination) bow lights are *always* white. Now, assume you see a white running light and nothing else. This tells you that it is on a boat that is anchored or running forward of you in the same approximate direction. Were the boat approaching you, its red or green light, or both, would be visible. Check the chart (page 62). If the approaching boat is larger than 26 feet or rigged under International Rules, you would also see a white light. Work out the possible situations yourself, and practice until your response is automatic. And right.

By the numbers

The final item of equipment is registration numbers, a universal requirement on United States and Canadian waters for undocumented boats having any propulsion machinery, regardless of type or horsepower. In the United States the Federal Boat Safety Act of 1971 calls for such boats to have a number "issued by the proper issuing authority in the State in which the vessel is principally used." If the state has a federally approved boat-numbering system, the proper issuing authority is some department of the state itself—the Conservation Department, the Bureau of Motor Vehicles, whatever the state has set up for this purpose (see list of state boating agencies on page 104). If the state does not have an approved numbering system, and at this writing (Summer of 1976) only Alaska, the District of Columbia, New Hampshire, and Washington do not, the Coast Guard is the proper issuing authority.

A powerboat whose principal use is on the high seas must be numbered by the state in which it is used when it is not on the high seas.

Each state must recognize the validity of a number issued by another state or by the Coast Guard for at least sixty days. (U.S. pleasure craft may enter Canada for up to twelve months under a permit you can get at any Canadian customs port-of-entry.)

The numbers, which must be at least three inches high, may be painted on or affixed to the forward half of the boat (the bow), and those must be the only numbers displayed there. They must read from left to right, be "plain vertical block characters" in a color that contrasts with the background, and be distinctly visible and legible.

Do not confuse registration numbers with "hull identification numbers." You are responsible for getting and displaying the former; the boatbuilder is responsible for providing and affixing the latter. You'll find the hull identification number on the outboard side of the transom above the waterline on all boats used or intended to be used on federally navigable waters. It consists of at least twelve consecutive characters which are not less than one-quarter inch high. The first three characters are a code for the builder's identity; it was assigned to that builder by the Coast Guard. The next five characters comprise that individ-

Running lights between sunset and sunrise

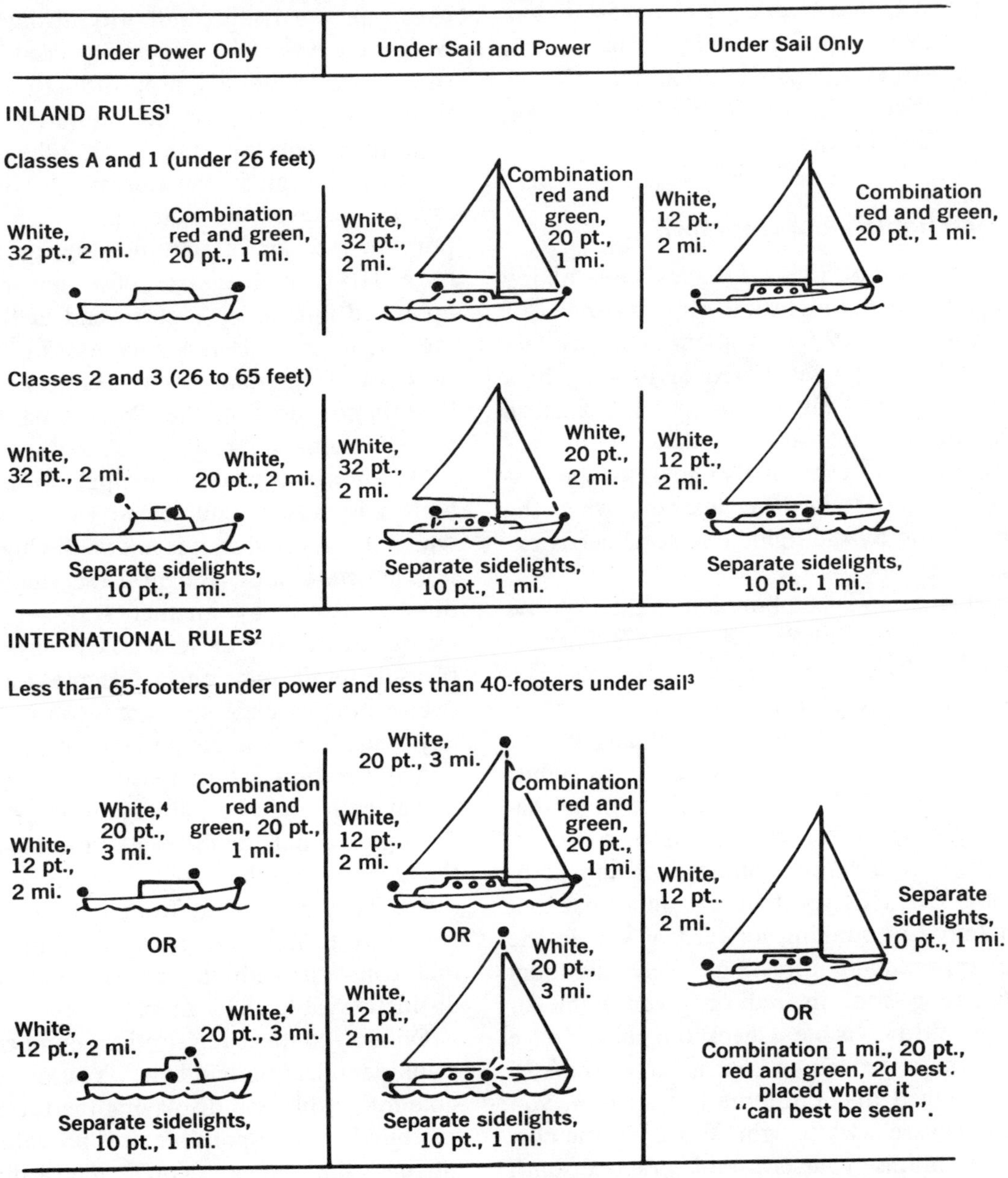

[1] These lights meet legal requirements on all navigable waters of the United States inside the high seas. On the Great Lakes a boat under sail alone need not show a stern light but, like sailboats everywhere, must show a white light to an approaching vessel.

[2] These lights, or alternatives provided for larger vessels, must be shown on the high seas; on inland navigable waters they may be used instead of the lights otherwise required.

[3] Powerboats from 65 feet to less than 150 feet must show a 20-point, white forward light visible for at least 5 miles and placed at least 20 feet above the hull; separate 10-point sidelights visible for at least 2 miles; and a white 12-point stern light visible for at least 2 miles. Sailboats 40 feet and larger must carry only the 10-point, 2-mile sidelights and white, 12-point, 2-mile stern light shown.

[4] Required to be in the "forepart of the vessel, where it can best be seen, and at a height above the gunwale (top edge of boat's side) of not less than 9 feet" unless the boat is less than 40 feet in length, in which case it need be only "not less than 3 feet" above the sidelights or the combination light.

Some combination lights (they show red to port, green to starboard) come with a jack staff, from which the skipper can fly his club or private signal (flag). (*Photo courtesy Perko.*)

ual hull's serial number. And the last four numbers tell you the month and year of the date of manufacture or, if the boat is "subject to a standard," the month and year of the date of certification.

Nor should you confuse registration with licensing. No demonstration of skill or knowledge is needed; only a completed application blank and the appropriate fee. Some states also call for proof of boat ownership—a bill of sale, for example. Applications, rates, and further information can be obtained from the sources listed on page 104. In Canada, boat registration is free; apply to any Customs and Excise Office.

Excluded from the numbering requirement are yachts which have been "documented." They receive official papers from the federal government—it used to be from the Bureau of Customs, now it is being handled by the Coast Guard—attesting to the documentation. The privilege is limited to yachts owned by U.S. citizens, or by corporations in which more than half the stock is owned by U.S. citizens, and which measure at least five net tons (most 35-footers and up). The principal benefit of documentation is for owners who hope to secure Preferred Ship Mortgage financing. This is because all financial transactions affecting ownership of a documented yacht may be recorded, and thereby establish an enforceable priority of liens, which understandably is how bankers prefer to do business.

There is no charge for documentation and if you are interested in the detailed procedure, pick up the pamphlet CG-177, *Yacht Admeasurement and Documentation* from your local Coast Guard office.

How much does it cost?

The horn aboard my 22-foot outboard cruiser is a hand-held packet consisting of a 4-inch, chromed-brass trumpet that screws onto a shaving-cream-size can of compressed freon gas. The going price for such a device is about $15; freon refills, about $3. A can should last three to four months in normal use. Its blast more than meets the minimum one-mile audibility required. So too does the pair of horns a friend of mine uses on his 38-foot cruiser, dazzlingly shined, elegantly styled 20-inch-long affairs costing $240. They are push-button, electrically operated, compressed air (a com-

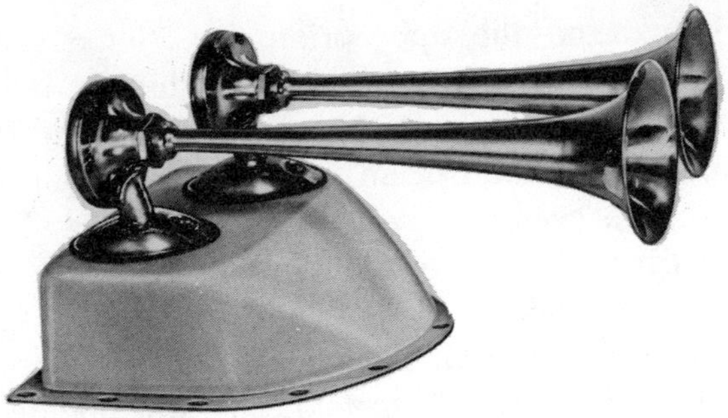

One way to manage the required "whistle" signals is with permanently installed air horns. The compressor for the pair here is contained in the waterproof housing beneath the chrome-over-brass trumpets. (*Photo courtesy Industrial Times Corp.*)

pressor is included in the price), de luxe horns. Between these examples is a plethora of models and price tags. And this is how it is with most marine equipment. Here is the range of prices at which you will find the other federally required items.

Backfire flame arrestors: these are mechanical devices that attach to the air intakes of carburetors to do what their name says; prices range from $15 to $45. As with all equipment *required to be Coast Guard-approved* (see chart on page 58), if the flame arrestor is not so designated, do not buy it for marine use. Approval is given to those products that meet the Coast Guard's minimum product specifications. It does *not* indicate differences in quality beyond this standard.

Ventilators: the vents called for here are those necessary to air the boat's bilges (lower portion of the boat's interior) to avoid the collection of volatile vapors, most notably from gasoline. You will need at least one vent for an intake and another for an exhaust. Ducts must be installed to lead from the openings to those areas where vapors are most apt to collect: the deepest part of the bilge that the fumes can reach. Flexible wire reinforced plastic tubing makes an easy-to-handle and, if impervious to moisture, acids, and oils, sufficiently durable duct. A 5-foot length with a 3-inch diameter sells for about $6. A pair of 3- to 4-inch (diameter of the vent's opening)

The more popular way to sound off on smaller boats is to use a hand-held horn that is actuated by compressed freon gas. One can should last through a season of weekending use, but it's inexpensive enough to keep an extra aboard.

chrome-plated brass ventilators sells for about $15. Prices rise with size to the motor-yacht types, which sell for about $150 each. The 3-inchers are popular on boats in the 20-foot or so category and are often installed through what are technically termed "covering boards" but are commonly called the "side decks" over the fuel tank area.

Federal regulations exclude completely open boats from having to install ventilators, but few powerboats meet the definition of an open boat. The exclusionary provision is intended to apply to boats having no enclosures in which explosive vapors might be trapped—an outboard-powered raft, for instance. If you have any doubt as to whether yours is an open boat or not, ventilate. The more the better.

Fog bells: usually cast in bronze or brass; fog bells sell for $10 to $27. A popular size

Flame arrestors—this model is made by Bendix—are required on the carburetors of inboard gasoline engines.

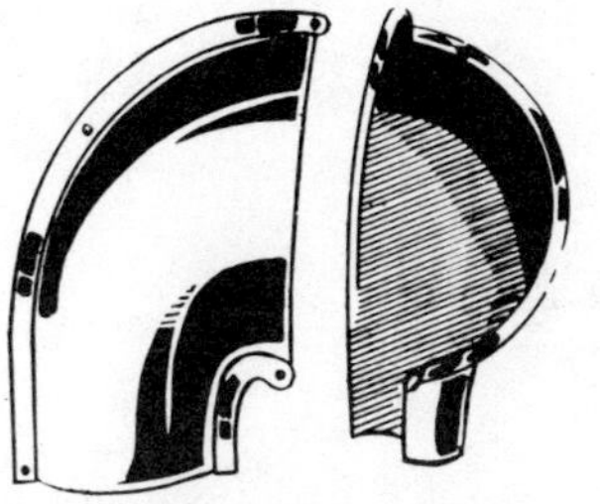

Popular on small boats are side-type air vents, installed through the side decks (the technical name for which is "covering boards") and secured to the sides of the cabin. Flexible ducting is then connected to the bottom of the vents and led to the lowest parts of the bilge.

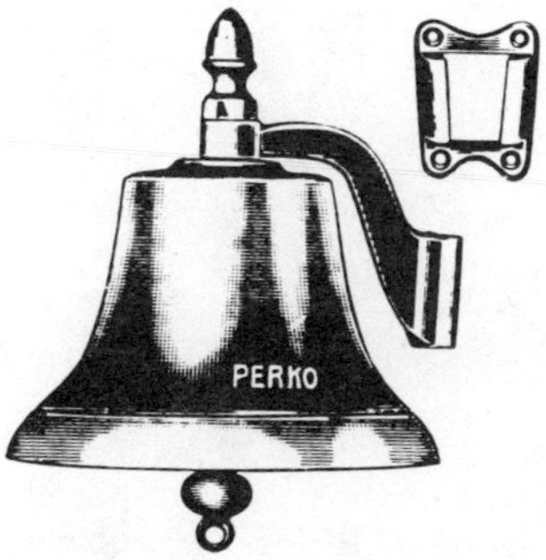

Fog bells are required on certain boats so that they can sound the proper signal when under way in fog. There are automatic fog-signal devices on the market, the cost of which of course is appreciably higher.

on pleasure boats is a bell having an extreme diameter of 6 to 8 inches.

Lifesavers: the generic name coined by Coast Guard regulations in 1973 for all marine lifesaving equipment of the preserver-vest-ring buoy variety is Personal Flotation Device, or PFD. *All recreational boats must carry at least one approved PFD for each person aboard.* Nothing prevents you from carrying more than is required. Or having additional lifesaving devices that are not Coast Guard approved.

Depending on what they are and what they have been designed to do, each Coast Guard-approved PFD comes under one of five categories, thusly:

Type I PFD: designed to turn an unconscious person from a face-down position to a vertical or slightly reclining position, and to provide more than 20 pounds of buoyancy. The various styles of life preservers, both the jacket type and the "bib" type, fall into this category. For my money, jackets buoy best. A kapok-filled adult jacket (for persons weighing more than 90 pounds) costs about $16, one filled with fibrous glass material, about $20. Figure on spending about $1 less for children's sizes of either type. Because life jackets are uncomfortable to wear out of the water, it generally is a battle to get the kids, and your non-swimming guests, to keep them on while aboard or at dockside. Insist.

Type II PFD: same as I, except that it need provide only 15½ pounds of buoyancy. These are the buoyant vests, manufactured in a variety of styles and colors, and using the same flotation filler as the jackets, but less of it. Vests come in three sizes: Adult, Child-Medium and Child-Small, with the weight ranges for the children's sizes conspicuously marked on the vest. Because they are smaller than jackets, they are somewhat more comfortable to wear, but they provide less buoyancy and, so, less safety. Figure on spending about $12 for an adult vest and about $1 or $2 less for a child's size.

Most children resist having to wear a personal flotation device. Insist anyhow. The responsibility for seeing that the correct PFDs are aboard is yours as skipper. The weight range for children's lifesaving devices is marked on all Coast Guard-approved PFDs. (*Photo by the author.*)

Type III PFD: designed to help keep a person who is conscious in a vertical or slightly reclining position and, like Type IIs, to provide at least 15½ pounds of buoyancy. Because there's no requirement for these devices to turn an unconscious wearer's face up, these devices are often light and comfortable, like some of the approved water-skiing harnesses (note: a towed water skier is counted as a person aboard for purposes of determining the minimum number of PFDs needed).

Type IV PFD: designed to be thrown and grabbed, not worn, and must provide at least 16½ pounds of buoyancy. Ring buoys come under this category, of course (one with a 30-inch diameter will stand you about $30), but by far the most popular Type IV device is the buoyant cushion. Filled with plastic foam, kapok, or fibrous glass material, cushions sell for about $10 each and are made in an almost endless variety of colors and motifs.

Type V PFD: heavy work vests are covered by this category, not usually approved for use on recreational boats.

Okay, what are you going to buy? You'll note from the foregoing chart of required equipment (see page 58), that if your boat is smaller than 16 feet you must have one Type I, II, III, or IV PFD for each person aboard. If the boat is 16 feet or larger, you must have one Type I, II, or III (all wearable) PFD for each person aboard *plus* at least one Type IV (throwable) in the boat. What I do is have one jacket (that's a Type I PFD) for everyone apt to be aboard plus at least one ring buoy and a scattering of buoyant cushions on the boat. That exceeds the legal requirement for any size of boat, but in stormy weather you and your guests will be glad you did.

Fire extinguishers: portable dry chemical (usually sodium bicarbonate) models in capacities (2½ to 3 pounds) that meet small-boat needs price out at $9 to $35, depending on the elaborateness of the casing and the trigger assembly. The dry chemical is the most common type found aboard small boats. Carbon dioxide extinguishers in five-pound capacities sell for $50 to $70 and are the next most commonly preferred aboard. Foam-filled extinguishers (content is a protein-based foam that expands 30 to 40 times in volume when released) sell for about $40 in a 2½-gallon size and are probably the least popular choice. The foam leaves a sticky mess when used and, compared with dry chemicals, is expensive. All these extinguishers operate on the same principle: they smother the flame. Combustion cannot continue without oxygen. Dry chemical, carbon dioxide, or foam all cut off the oxygen supply. Carbon dioxide does it the fastest and cleanest, dry chemical the most cheaply, foam the most messily. Each is effective enough to receive Coast Guard approval. A useful booklet on the subject is available (75 cents) from the National Fire Protection As-

The PFD most often chosen by small-boat skippers, either to meet the legal requirements on a boat that's smaller than 16 feet or to have in addition to other PFDs on larger boats, is the seat cushion, adequate as long as it is kept up to snuff. When too many heavyweights sit on them a bit too often, however, cushions tend to split their vinyl seams and thereby lose both their buoyancy and Coast Guard approval.

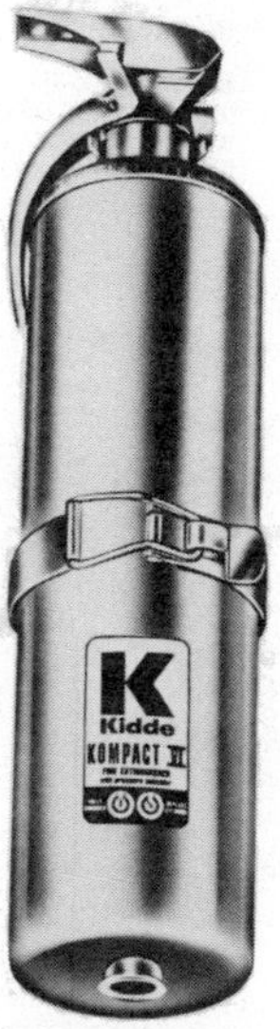

Compact fire extinguishers designed for marine use (which means they are rustproof and packaged to meet federal requirements) are, like PFDs, reasonably priced for the protection they buy; having one or two more aboard than the law requires makes good sense. Check each unit's pressure gauge from time to time to insure the extinguisher is ready for action, and learn in advance how it's used.

sociation, 60 Batterymarch St., Boston, Mass. 02110; ask for its NFPA Standard No. 302 for Motor Craft.

Whichever you choose, learn immediately how the model you purchase is used so that, should a fire erupt, you can put the extinguisher into operation without fumbling. They almost all are activated by squeezing a trigger; but they almost all, to avoid having the extinguisher go off accidentally, have a locking device whose operation should be mastered.

Most models are sold with a bulkhead mounting bracket. Consider its mounting location carefully. Where is a fire most apt to occur? Statistics tells us in the galley and in the fuel compartment. Should this happen aboard your boat, will you be able to reach the extinguisher? Only you can say, since it depends upon the layout of your boat. A typically ideal arrangement is to mount one extinguisher near the galley stove and another at the steering station. Generally one or the other extinguisher will be accessible in an emergency. This plan calls for at least two extinguishers, of course, but it is a maximum safety we are pursuing, not simply compliance with a minimum standard. The following chapter should make this notion clearer.

(Photo courtesy Bahamas News Bureau.)

Chapter 7
EQUIPPING THE BOAT—II

We have seen in the previous chapter what the law says must be aboard. It is not enough. There is no express federal provision for an anchor, compass, first-aid kit, fenders, or tools, to name some gear you'll want for safety's sake. Other items will be desired for the convenience or luxury they provide; I mean, besides a "first mate," such things as fishing-rod holders, dish racks, and a cooler if no icebox or refrigerator is aboard. Your inventory should be in keeping with: (1) the size of the boat you use; (2) the activity you put it to; and (3) the waters you ply. In one of the many booklets the Coast Guard publishes on recreational boating safety, there is a CG-recommended list of additional safety equipment. I have modified that list slightly, adding items I think important, deleting some which, though possibly worthwhile, are for various practical reasons seldom used, and here and there increasing applicability. Use as indicated by "E," essential; "D" desirable; "O," optional; and "X," no application.

1. A boat hook is a slender, wood, metal, or plastic pole 4 to 6 feet long, with a small hook jutting out from beneath one blunted end. It is used to fend off, grab on, and pick up in situations ranging from docking to "hat overboard." Telescoping models simplify stowage. A cork or rubber cap over the hook's point will prevent mishaps aboard. Place a cork over fishhooks and gaffs, incidentally, for the same reason.

2. Official-chart sources and information on the use of charts appear in Chapters 10 and 11. I can suggest no better boating purchase: charts are inexpensive, incredibly accurate, and chockablock with handy information. Because they are continually revised, use only the latest. Included are the locations of federal anchorage grounds, sunken ships, fish traps, buoys, lighthouses, landmarks, and pleasure-boat facilities, the last-named especially on charts in small-craft series. Also given are water depths, bridge clearances, mileage scales, the means for deriving compass headings, and bottom condition.

3. To seventeenth-century sailors, *defenders* were strips of wood or bundles of wood or bundles of rope hung over a vessel's side to prevent chafe. Today's shortened pleasure-boat fenders (Latin *fendere,* "to beat off,") are often inexpensive chunks of soft plastic threaded with line permanently looped at one end to hook over a deck cleat, and the costlier but longer-lasting air-filled fenders, usually made of rubber. Stenciling your boat's name on the fender will help discourage theft.

4. Many pre-packaged first-aid kits contain too little, a condition often discovered too

Additional Safety Equipment

Item	Class A			Class 1			Class 2			Class 3			Approximate Prices
	Open waters	*Semi-protected*	*Protected*	*Open waters*	*Semi-protected*	*Protected*	*Open waters*	*Semi-protected*	*Protected*	*Open waters*	*Semi-protected*	*Protected*	
Anchor(s)	E	E	E	E	E	E	E	E	E	E	E	E	$9 to $260
Bailing device (pump, scoop-type bailer, etc.)	E	E	E	E	E	E	E	E	E	E	E	E	scoops, $1 and up; manual pumps, $9–12 and up; automatic pumps, $32 and up
Battery box	E	E	E	E	E	E	D	D	D	O	O	O	$5 to $10
Binoculars	D	D	O	D	D	O	D	D	D	D	D	D	$35 and up
Boat hook[1]	D	D	D	D	D	D	E	E	E	E	E	E	$5.50 to $20
Boat shoes	E	E	E	E	E	E	E	E	E	E	E	E	$12 to $135
Bow rail	X	X	X	D	D	D	E	E	E	E	E	E	$70 and up
Charts[2]	E	E	D	E	E	E	E	E	E	E	E	E	75¢ and up
Compass	E	E	D	E	E	E	E	E	E	E	E	E	$19 and up
Distress signals	E	E	E	E	E	E	E	E	E	E	E	E	hand flares, about $2.50 each; flare gun kit, about $50; distress flag, about $3
Extra food, water, fuel	E	D	O	E	D	O	E	D	O	E	D	O	at least $10 worth
Fenders[3]	D	D	D	D	D	D	D	D	D	D	D	D	$3 and up
First-aid kit, manual[4]	E	E	E	E	E	E	E	E	E	E	E	E	$10 and up
Flashlight	E	E	E	E	E	E	E	E	E	E	E	E	$1.50 and up
Foul weather clothes	E	D	D	E	D	D	E	D	D	E	D	D	$20 and up
Gas fume blowers[5]	O	O	O	D	D	D	D	D	D	E	E	E	$18 and up

[1] See page 69 for meanings of letter symbols, and pages 69, 72, and 73 for explanations of numbered items.

Item	Class A			Class 1			Class 2			Class 3			Approximate Prices
	Open waters	*Semi-protected*	*Protected*	*Open waters*	*Semi-protected*	*Protected*	*Open waters*	*Semi-protected*	*Protected*	*Open waters*	*Semi-protected*	*Protected*	
Gas fume detector[6]	O	O	O	O	O	O	D	D	D	D	D	D	$85 and up
Lantern	O	O	O	D	D	D	D	D	D	D	D	D	$8 and up
Megaphone or hailer	O	O	O	D	D	D	D	D	D	D	D	D	$5 and up
Mooring lines	E	E	E	E	E	E	E	E	E	E	E	E	½″ dia. nylon from 21¢ a foot
Paddle or oar	E	E	E	D	D	D	X	X	X	X	X	X	$9 and up
Pelorus[7]	O	O	O	D	D	D	D	D	D	D	D	D	$12 and up
Portable radio	E	E	E	E	E	E	E	E	E	E	E	E	(almost all prices)
Radar	X	X	X	X	X	X	O	O	O	D	D	D	$1800 and up
Radar reflector[8]	D	D	O	D	D	O	D	D	O	D	D	O	$9 and up
Radio direction finder[9]	O	O	X	D	D	O	D	D	O	D	D	O	$100 and up
Radiotelephone	D	O	O	D	D	D	D	D	D	D	D	D	$200 and up
Ring buoy (extra)	D	D	D	D	D	D	D	D	D	D	D	D	$12 and up
Screws, bolts, etc.	E	E	E	E	E	E	E	E	E	E	E	E	assortment kit from $16
Sounding device[10]	D	D	D	D	D	D	E	E	E	E	E	E	lead lines, $11 and up; elec. depth sounder, $100 and up
Spare batteries	D	D	D	D	D	D	D	D	D	D	D	D	flashlight size, 25¢
Spare parts (engine, lights, etc.)	E	D	D	E	D	D	E	E	D	E	E	D	about $40
Tachometer(s)	D	D	D	D	D	D	D	D	D	D	D	D	$50 and up
Tools and chest	E	E	E	E	E	E	E	E	E	E	E	E	about $50

late. Buy the most complete kit you can find, preferably put up in a waterproof container, and then ask your doctor what to add. Promptly replace what is used or old. Also, unless you are skilled in first-aid procedures, learn them now, and keep a reference aboard. One of the most comprehensive manuals is *Standard First Aid and Personal Safety*, published by the American Red Cross; its latest edition (1973) is available for $1.95 from local chapters and elsewhere.

As at home, keep the first-aid kit aboard out of the reach of children, but show everyone cruising with you where it is.

5. Blowers are discussed in Chapter 4.

6. Gasoline-fume detectors buzz, ring, whistle, or light when fumes are present. The warning component is installed topside, the connecting "sensing" part, below. Used with discretion, detectors are a valuable aid. Like bilge blowers, they are not meant to replace your control—*you* should sniff the bilge, after the boat is fueled—but to supplement it. Other available detection devices that can be installed aboard warn of water in the bilge, improper oil pressure, unsynchronized engines in twin-screw setups, and even corrosion of underwater hull fittings.

7. A look at the compass tells you, assuming that error is corrected, the course your boat is on but not where you are. If with the compass you could sight two charted objects, you could ascertain their bearing and plot the data on the appropriate chart. The point of intersection "fixes" your position. But it is often inconvenient or impossible to use the boat's

Among the more versatile items aboard is the boat hook, used to fend off, grab on, and pick up. Product here is boat hook on one end, paddle on the other; it's marketed by Woolsey Marine Paints.

Before docking make it a habit to put out fenders. Three to a side will usually suffice if the fenders are large enough for your craft.

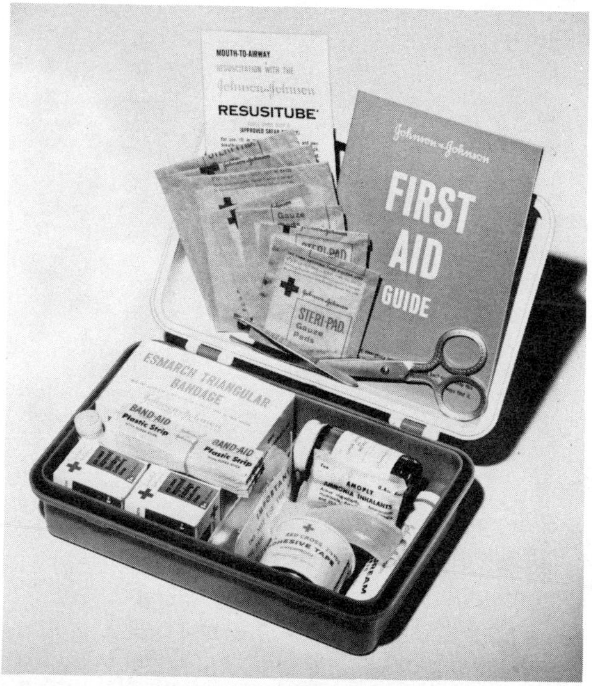

Tailor the contents of prepackaged first-aid kits—insulin? Excedrin? diuretics?—to meet the potential needs of those persons expected to be aboard. Most importantly, learn basic first-aid procedures now, before they are needed.

Get lost ashore and you generally can ask someone how to get to where you are going. Get lost afloat and the only help you may have is your compass. Buy a good one, large enough to hold steady. Small, dinky compasses are useless aboard because the motion of the boat makes it virtually impossible to read the card.

compass for sighting: it is installed too low or its spherical dome prevents you from viewing across its girth. The solution is easy: rig a compass "remote," the simple pelorus. This is a flat reproduction of a compass card (face) and a pair of sighting vanes; both the card and the vanes turn freely. To use the pelorus, just align its card with the boat's compass card, sight the objects with the sighting vanes, and take their bearings.

8. Not yet in popular use—unfortunately—the radar reflector is only a hunk of metal that will "blip up" distinctly on a searching vessel's radar screen. Large metal craft do not need them; their hull material and their hulk help to insure an echo. Small boats may be overlooked, especially fiberglass and wood-hulled ones that will not bounce a blip back, which is why raising a metal reflector is recommended. Collapsible models are easiest to stow.

9. A radio direction finder (RDF) provides an electronic way to determine position and bearings. It receives characteristic signals transmitted by various radio beacons whose locations are known. You tune in the beacon you want, much as you tune in a particular program on a conventional radio, and by manipulating some dials if the set is not automatic (ADF) you determine the transmitter's bearing. A second beacon bearing provides a fix (see item 7 above) and a third will help insure accuracy. By following a single signal—this is called "homing in"—you can slice a straight path to the transmitter.

10. The purpose of a sounding device is to determine the depth of water beneath the boat, primarily to avoid running aground but, because water depths are shown on official charts, sometimes also to navigate. The two common types are (1) a lead line; and (2) an electronic echo sounder, or depth finder. The former consists of a weight, traditionally lead, attached to the end of a line whose length is

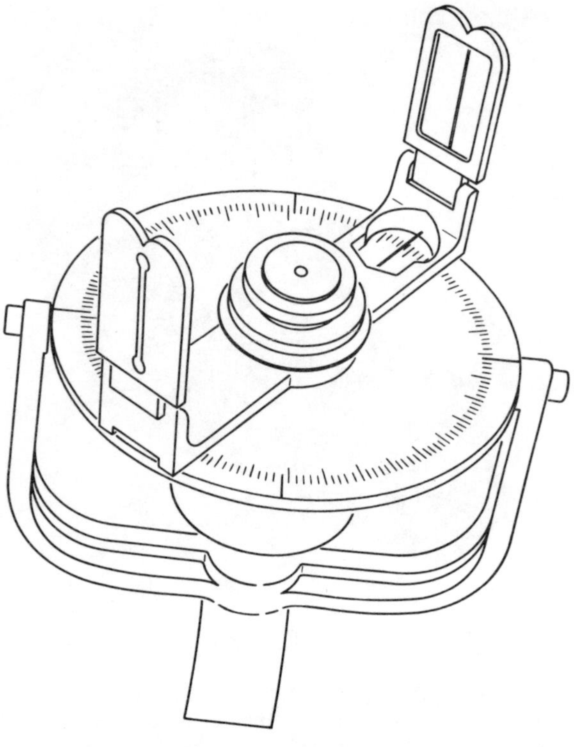

One of the many kinds of peloruses on the market. Prices range from just a few dollars to as much as $95, depending on the elaborateness of the device.

Radar is being designed in remarkably compact modules for the small-boat market—well, for the small-cruiser market, in any event. Model here, Decca's Super 050, has 12-mile range with 500-yard interval calibrating rings on the ½ and 1½ mile scales for better close-in ranging. About $2,800.

Zenith's combination radio direction finder (RDF) and standard AM radio weighs a little over 5 pounds and is operated on C batteries. Price ranges in the $100 area.

Another type of RDF is this Ray Jeff automatic model (ADF), which searches out and positions the radio signal you want. Includes AM, FM, and VHF/FM bands and operates off boat's 12-volt power supply or eight 1.5-volt batteries. About $430.

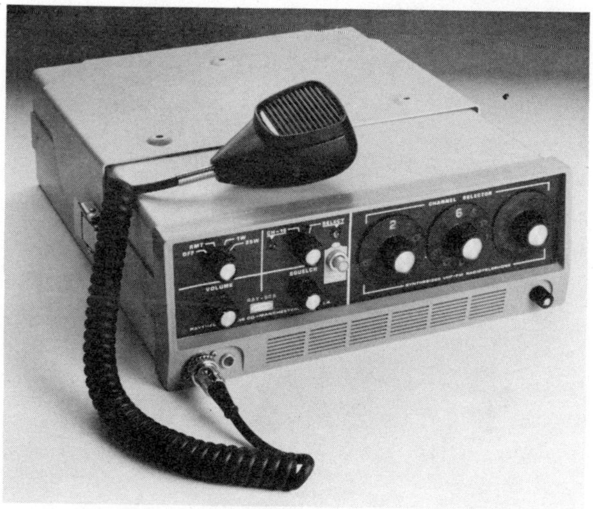

Model 50A VHF/FM Raytheon radiotelephone has 25-watt input, 56 transmit, and 96 receive channels, sells for about $700.

marked at regular intervals. Lowering the line overboard until the weight touches bottom reveals the depth. In growing use is the electronic depth-finder, which does the work for you. Impulses are emitted and the time they take to return is measured and translated into feet, or water depth—all electronically and instantly. With practice you can learn to read schools of passing fish.

Convenience and luxury

Obviously I can only hint at what equipment might fall into these categories; finances, imagination, and inclination will have to decide. A contributor to *Motor Boating* once wrote, "If it folds flat and won't rust, buy it," which is as good a guide as can be devised. Specialized activity, of course, entails its own special gear: scuba diving, for instance, and water skiing, deep-sea fishing, marine photography, racing, camping, and so on. But for posh comfort aboard, the marine market brims with such delights as air conditioners, heaters, windlasses (automatic anchor hoists), automatic pilots, ice-cube-making machines, Deepfreezes. . . . The list is practically endless, but before buying ask—"Can I stow it? Will it rust?"

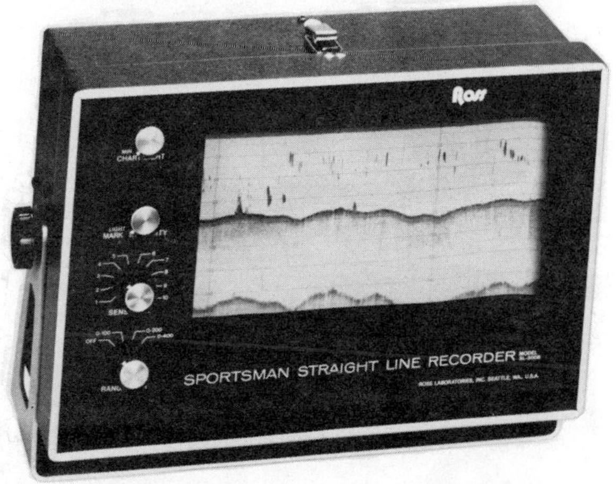

Ross Sportsman depth recorder/fish finder has rated range of 300 feet with sensitivity enough, its publicity flak says, to record even a single fish at up to 125 feet. Price is about $750. Recorders that make paper records of the readings, such as this model, are more costly than direct read-out recorders, which begin at about $125. Serious fishermen who want a permanent record of bottom contours in order to get back to where the fish were, for example, prefer the former; cruisingmen who simply want to know how much water there is beneath the hull choose the latter. Recorders can be used as an aid in navigation as well, since readings, allowing for tide, ought to square with the depth listings on the corresponding nautical charts.

The Auxiliary exam

There is still another way to insure that your boat is properly equipped: request a free exam from your local Coast Guard Auxiliary. The CGA is strictly a voluntary, civilian organization dedicated to public service. Your local Coast Guard district office can tell you where the nearest CGA inspection team is located.

If your powerboat passes the CGA exam it will be awarded a decal. Put it on your boat's windshield; it often heads off a random boarding inspection the Coast Guard might otherwise make. Besides the foregoing federal requirements, some of which are expanded upon

Automatic pilot, or "iron Mike," for long open-water cruising is hard luxury to beat. Note, it does not excuse the skipper from having to maintain a constant lookout! Model shown is Unipas 2000, designed for boats 30 feet and larger. (List price is $1,355.) What you do is put your boat on the heading you want, rotate the unit's magnetic heading selector to the corresponding course, and switch the auto pilot on. Manually moving the steering wheel overrides the automatic system.

Flashing light on this small instrument permits easy synchronization of twin-engine setup, yielding improved fuel economy and smoother performance. Model shown is Judson's pedestal mount, about $50.

below, your boat will need all the following, which in most instances is more than the law requires, to earn its decal:

☐ PERSONAL FLOTATION DEVICES—There must be at least as many approved personal flotation devices, of the type required for the class of boat, as there are berths. A boat with less than two bunks must have at least two approved personal flotation devices aboard. Personal flotation devices must be readily accessible.

☐ FIRE EXTINGUISHERS—All powerboats under 26 feet, whether or not they are equipped with a fixed fire extinguishing system, must carry one hand portable fire extinguisher of approved type.

☐ NAVIGATION LIGHTS must be of a configuration specified for the class of boat and must be operative and fully visible through the required arc.

☐ DISTRESS FLARE—All powerboats must carry a distress flare for emergency signaling.

☐ GALLEY STOVE—If carried, the galley stove must be securely mounted so that it cannot shift position. Stoves must be installed so that no flammable materials in the vicinity can be ignited. Any of the common types of fuel may be used *except* gasoline.

☐ PERMANENTLY INSTALLED FUEL TANKS must be securely mounted so that they cannot shift position.

☐ FUEL TANK VENT—A vent terminating outboard of the hull and compartments must lead to each permanently installed fuel tank.

☐ FUEL TANK FILL PIPE—Fill pipes leading to permanently installed fuel tanks must fit into a filling plate located on deck

Boat, or deck, shoes, which should not be confused with sneakers, are a must for safety aboard. Soles grip even wet, sloping decks. Fashionable oxford, loafer, men's, women's, and children's styles, are available in leather and canvas. (*Photo courtesy Randy Boatshu.*)

in such a manner that fuel spills easily drain overboard.

☐ PORTABLE FUEL TANKS AND SPARE FUEL CONTAINERS—Tanks and containers which exceed 7 gallons are not classed as portable tanks, and must meet all requirements for permanently installed tanks. Tanks and spare fuel containers of less than 7 gallons must be tight and sufficiently sturdy to withstand ordinary usage. Glass or other breakable materials may not be used for portable fuel tanks or containers.

☐ CARBURETOR DRIP PAN—A drip pan must be installed under all side draft or up draft carburetors not provided with an effective pump.

☐ BACKFIRE FLAME CONTROL—All inboard powerboats, regardless of date of construction or engine installation, must meet current federal requirements for backfire flame control.

☐ WHISTLE OR SOUND-PRODUCING DEVICE—All Class A boats must carry a whistle or sound-producing device capable of producing a blast of 2 seconds or more duration and audible at least ½ mile.

Tuna towers, usually of anodized aluminum, sell for about $700 and up, depending on height; they put the pilot up high for better spotting of lazing swords, feeding gulls, telltale fins, etc.

☐ VENTILATION—All powerboats regardless of class or date of construction must meet the current federal requirements for ventilation.

☐ ELECTRICAL INSTALLATION—Wiring must be in good condition and properly installed. There should be no open knife switches located in the bilge.

☐ ANCHOR AND ANCHOR LINE—The

Even school tuna, let alone great whites, marlin, and yellowfins, are best fished for from a fighting chair for the fisherman's comfort and security. About $500.

Jigsaw them yourself or buy ready-made at most waterside stores; rod racks allow for convenient stowage aboard. Secure them overhead or along bulkheads in the cabin.

Combination bow pulpit and anchor windlass (a device that raises the anchor automatically) is sold by Ideal for about $775. Switches can be installed at the helm or bridge or on the forward deck—or at all three stations.

boat must be equipped with an adequate anchor and line of suitable length for the locality.

☐ GENERAL CONDITION—The vessel must be in good over-all condition, the hull sound, fuel lines intact and properly installed. The maximum HP rating contained on the capacity plate must not be exceeded. The decal will not be awarded to a vessel which is not generally shipshape and in seaworthy condition.

☐ POWERBOATS under 16 feet must carry the following additional equipment: a pump, or bailer, and a paddle or an oar.

While not cause for withholding the decal, the Auxiliary strongly recommends the following standards:

☐ Through hull fittings should have shut-off valves or wooden plugs accessible for use.

☐ Fuel lines should lead from the top of the tank and be equipped with shut-off valves at the tank and engine.

☐ Auxiliary generators should have separate fuel tanks.

☐ All switches located in the bilges should be designed for submerged use.

☐ Distress signaling equipment should be carried on every boat.

☐ A manual bilge pump should be carried on every boat irrespective of any mechanical pumping devices.

☐ Handrails should be secured with through bolts.

☐ Spare canisters should be carried for horns or whistles which operate from compressed gas.

☐ Spare batteries and spare bulbs should be carried for battery-operated lights.

☐ A fully equipped first-aid kit should be carried in every boat.

☐ Have tools and spare parts on board in usable condition.

☐ The safe loading plate affixed at the time of manufacture should be legible and the load capacities indicated thereon should not be exceeded.

(*Photo by the author.*)

Chapter 8
HANDLING THE BOAT

Handling a boat calls for (1) *logical* responses to situations; and (2) *legally* required ones. Sometimes they are identical; sometimes they are not—as when one alternative seems as prudent as another. Where these are alternatives, especially in situations where risk of collision might exist, legislators have decided the issue, in this way producing *predictability* and, with it, increased safety afloat. Broadly, federal boat-handling regulations in the United States are called the "Rules of the Road," and it is to them we turn first.

Rules of the watery road

There are four regional federal sets of rules: Great Lakes (contained in Coast Guard pamphlet CG-172); Western River (CG-184); Inland and International (both in CG-169). The Western rivers include most of the Mississippi and its tributaries, the Red River of the North, and the Atchafalaya River above its junction with the Plaquemine-Morgan City alternate waterway. Inside of the high seas (see page 59) on waters other than the Western rivers and the Great Lakes, the Inland Rules must be followed. Because these affect the majority of boatmen and because all sets of rules are essentially similar, the examples that follow are based on Inland Rules.

When powerboats are approaching each other from opposite or nearly opposite directions (as below), each must pass on the port (left) side of the other after either has given a short (one-second) whistle blast to indicate

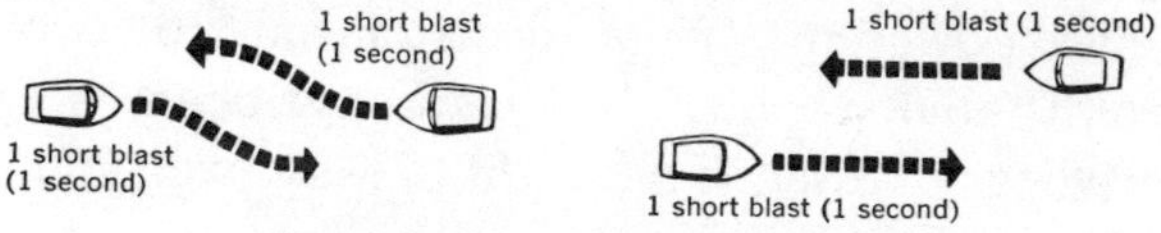

Passing in "head-on" situations.

this intent, and the other has promptly responded with an identical signal.

When the courses of the two boats are so far to starboard (right) of each other (as below) as not to be in a head-on or nearly head-on situation, the boats must pass starboard-to-starboard after exchanging two one-second

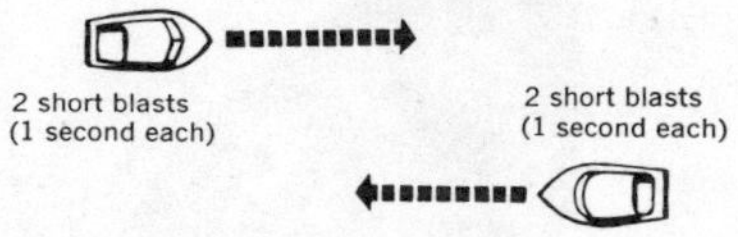

whistle signals. In narrow channels, however—a 300-foot-wide channel has been held to be narrow—powerboats are required to keep to the starboard side of the channel, thus passing port-to-port, when it is safe to do so. If, at night, you see both the red and green running lights of another vessel, you are probably in a head-on situation, and you should signal and maneuver accordingly.

Governing a crossing situation is this refreshingly brief "starboard hand" rule:

> When two powerboats are crossing, so as to involve risk of collision, the vessel which has the other on her own starboard side shall keep out of the way of the other.

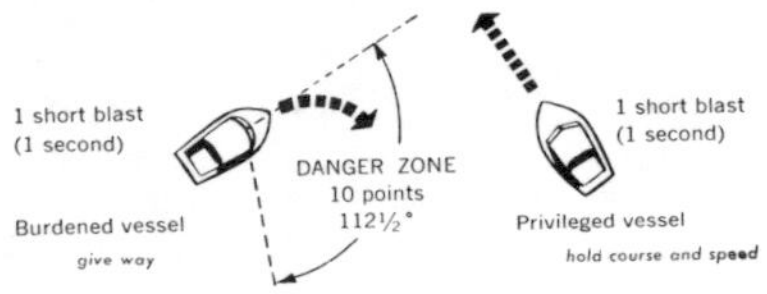

Crossing situations.

To distinguish a "crossing" vessel, especially from an "overtaking" one, the point system used in describing running lights (page 62) does double duty: every vessel approaching your powerboat from dead ahead to two points abaft (behind) the starboard beam is a privileged vessel; it has right of way over you. "Beam" in this sense means the center of the boat, a location halfway between bow and stern. Since there are 8 points from bow to beam, you have 10 points in all to watch on your starboard side. Some call this area the dee-zee or Danger Zone. The skipper approaching from within your Danger Zone not only may hold his course and speed but is under a duty to do so. You, as skipper of the "burdened" boat, must give way by swinging your boat to starboard to pass astern of the privileged vessel, or by slowing, stopping, or reversing—whichever is safest. Because of their greater maneuverability in crossing situations, powerboats must generally yield right of way to boats under sail alone. The whistle signal exchange, illustrated in the crossing situation (left), is not mandatory.

If at night you can see the *green* running light of another boat, and not its red one, you have the right of way. If you can see only its red light, the other powerboat has the right of way. If you can see the boat but neither its red nor green lights, and you appear to be gaining on it, you are probably an overtaking vessel.

Every boat about to be overtaken is a privileged one. Every boat overtaking another vessel from any direction greater than two points abaft the latter's beam—which is why the latter's colored lights will not be visible at night—is a burdened one with the duty of "keeping out of the way" until past and clear. Two one-second blasts indicate the overtaking skipper's intent to pass on the slower vessel's port side; one one-second toot, its starboard. If the privileged boat responds with an identical signal, the burdened boat can pass accordingly, swinging wide to keep clear. In no case should the privileged boat "attempt to cross the bow or crowd upon the course of the passing vessel." Because by day you will not have running lights to guide you, there may sometimes be doubt as to whether you are a crossing or an overtaking boat. When this happens, you are required to assume you are overtaking.

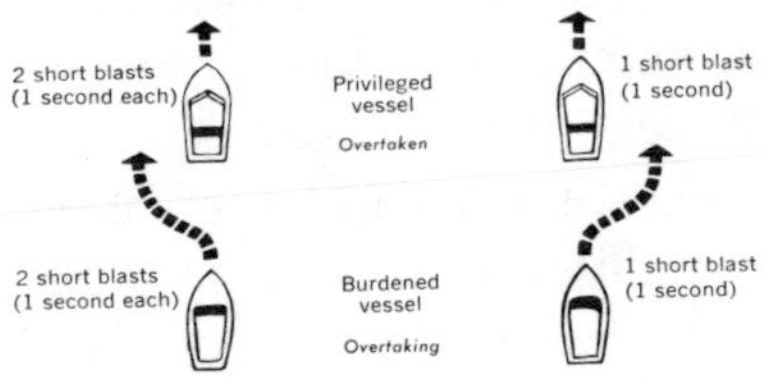

Overtaking situations.

Whistle stops

Whistle signals are seldom given with a whistle. Regrettably, they are seldom given at all, by pleasure boatmen at least, but when they are it is usually a horn that is used.

With one exception, a whistle signal must be answered with an identical signal. The holdout occurs when the responding boatman thinks the contemplated maneuver unsafe or impossible, or when he does not understand the other skipper's intention. He responds with the "danger" signal—four or more rapid, one-second blasts. In this event, each participating skipper is required to stop or reverse his vessel and continue on only after an agreement is reached, evidenced by an exchange of identical signals.

Whistle signals are to be initiated as soon as practicable when the crafts come in sight of each other. When approaching a bend around which visibility is obstructed, however, a vessel when it comes within one-half mile of the bend must sound a two-second blast, to be answered by any vessel within hearing. Then, if there is a response, conventional passing signals are to be exchanged immediately.

Thick-weather signals

Whistle signals, we have seen, are exchanged when boats are in sight of each other. What happens when visibility is blocked by weather rather than distance? Fog signals are what happens—in fog, of course, but also in heavy mists, snows, and rains. Powerboats under way are required to sound a four- to six-second whistle blast at least every minute. At anchor, powerboats must ring a fog *bell* rapidly for about five seconds at least every minute, unless in a special anchorage area (see page 60); here, 65-footers and under are excused from having to sound any signal at all.

Thick-weather speed

Just how fast does the law permit you to cruise in the foul weather conditions described above? The applicable Inland Rule fixes the limit flexibly at a "moderate speed," adding without appreciable helpfulness "having careful regard to the existing circumstances and conditions." Your speed should be such as will permit you to stop within less than half the distance of visibility, in this way averting risk of collision. Try stopping a few times. Throttle down to the conditions. In court cases, seven knots has been ruled moderate; three knots, too much! Your range of visibility at the time is the controlling factor.

If you hear a fog signal that appears to have come from somewhere forward of your boat's beam, you must stop your boat if it is safe to do so, and then navigate with added caution until there is no further risk of collision.

Discretion the better part

A powerboat under way is never excused from proper lights, signals, and a lookout. There is, however, one qualification to the rest of the navigation rules—they may be disregarded if necessary "to avoid immediate danger." Stubborn adherence to a rule, as one court put it, "is sometimes culpable fault." Never disregard a rule lightly; the circumstances must justify the departure. Inconvenience or a mere possibility of danger are not enough: a real and immediate risk of danger must exist, a rare situation. Remember the latitude you have but do not abuse it. Too, as said earlier, the four sets of *rules* are similar, not identical. Mostly the differences cope with local needs. You must know what is called for on your waters (see page 81). "Rules of the Road" pamphlets may be obtained free from any Coast Guard Marine Inspection Office. Vessels larger than 65 feet in length must carry a current copy aboard.

From fledgling to salt

The balance of the basic boat-handling maneuvers, that is, those not spelled out by law, should be logical responses to the situation, nothing fancier or more mysterious. True, the more knowledge you possess about the controlling elements the sharper your reactions will be. It is this knowledge that distinguishes the old salt. He can look at a *mare's tail* and know when and from where the winds will come. He can smell land miles off. He can tell the water's depth by its color and *cat's paws,* the set and drift of the current by the way a buoy heels. But he cut his teeth at sea; you probably did not. Nevertheless you have an edge—your modern boat, compact, powerful, highly maneuverable, fitted out with devices that sum up in moments what the salt needed years to learn. Practice will give you polish, but ordinary sense will permit you to begin with safety, will permit you to enjoy almost immediately the countless pleasures that boating offers.

It is beyond the scope of this volume to detail fully the steps in docking, anchoring, and fair and foul weather running. Other, fatter texts do this aptly, the best of which is *Piloting, Seamanship and Small Boat Handling* by the late Charles F. Chapman. But the nub of safe handling in all those boating activities can be held to this simple statement: go slowly, and look where you are going. Take docking, for example:

The best practice in docking, as in anchoring, is to come up to your destination with your boat headed into the wind or current, whichever is stronger. Besides checking your speed, this will dissipate the force of the element equally about your hull, pushing it to neither side. Suppose, instead, you approach with the wind (or current) astern or abeam. If you are moving quickly you will slam into the dock or skid past it. If you are moving slowly you have time to observe what is happening to your boat and to adjust direction or speed accordingly. Before you go out, devote a few hours to docking—just back and forth, back and forth—until it comes easily. You will have learned more than how to dock your boat, you will know how it responds to so much throttle, so much wind, so much sea; and you will have accomplished all this in complete safety. If you went slowly. If you looked where you were going.

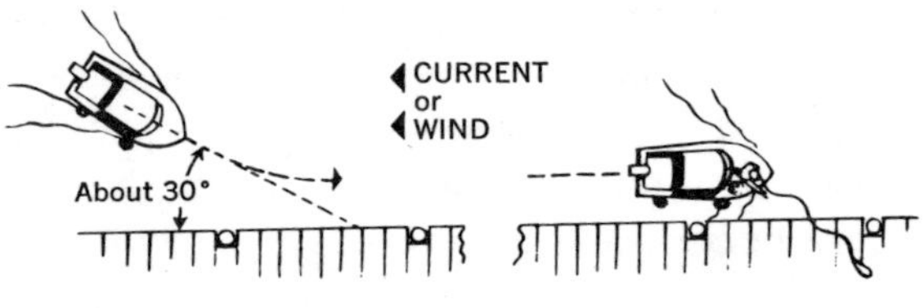

Soon "it" becomes "she"

Choose promising days and quiet waters for your boating until you acquire both skill in handling and confidence in your boat. Get a weather report before shoving off—and stay put if the forecast is gray. A hurricane is rough for any skipper in any vessel. How much less dirty the weather must be before a *seasoned* boatman should leave shore depends on the size and seaworthiness of his boat. If

Before you try open-throttle running in a chop, be sure you have mastered the basics of boat handling. This takes time, patience, and practice. (*Photo by Roland Rose, Bahamas Ministry of Tourism.*)

friends egg you on when reason holds you back, resist, preach patience, wait. Suggest a boat cleanup instead.

When you are afloat, observe the rules of the road, good manners, the way your boat behaves, its rhythm, its odors, its sounds. Soon "it" becomes "she"; you feel her. A strange sound, a foreign smell, an unexpected motion warns that something is different and perhaps amiss. Soon you can dock with dexterity, swing your boat on a dime, throttle her sensitively in following seas and violent inlets. You quarter each wave just so, without pounding, without broaching. Soon, but not immediately. Until then your safety, and the safety of those who are in your care, derives more from your caution than your skill. Go slowly and look where you are going.

Making safety a habit

Good boating habits can be developed easily, especially in the early stage of your boating career. Some boatmen make effective use of a checklist, not unlike those used by airplane pilots before takeoff, to be sure nothing important is neglected. The idea has much to recommend it. If it is executed by two or more persons—with your spouse? your kids?—you help them to acquire, painlessly, safe boating habits and fundamental boating knowledge. A checklist for getting under way should read something like this:

Getting under way

- ☐ You haven't invited too many people.
- ☐ The boat is free of dangerous fumes (sniff and see).
- ☐ Switch on exhaust blowers.
- ☐ Open hatches, windows, doors as you like.
- ☐ There is not too much water in the bilge.
- ☐ There are enough approved Personal Flotation Devices aboard for adults and children.
- ☐ Show new guests the location of PFDs, extinguishers, first-aid kit, distress signals, and the head, and instruct them on the use of each.
- ☐ There is enough fuel and oil.
- ☐ Fuel lines are connected to the outboard motors.
- ☐ The horn works.
- ☐ All other necessary equipment is aboard.
- ☐ See that you have boat registration certificate and proper charts aboard.
- ☐ Beverage, food, and ice are aboard if desired.
- ☐ Latest forecast is for reasonable boating weather.
- ☐ Distribute weight so that boat trims well.
- ☐ Warm up the engine(s).
- ☐ Switch off the exhaust blowers.
- ☐ Determine surrounding current (the way a buoy is heeling will tell you), wind (note the direction in which flags, moored boats, smoke are being blown), and sea conditions (merely look at what is happening to the water surface).
- ☐ Secure any potentially hazardous loose gear.
- ☐ Nothing has been forgotten on the dock.
- ☐ The engines are running smoothly.
- ☐ Cast off (or take in) the mooring lines.
- ☐ Take in the fenders.
- ☐ Leave slowly.

Now that you are under way, with your guests settled and the kids clamoring for soda pop, there are a few important items to which your attention should periodically and regularly be drawn. A checklist for these reads as follows:

While under way

- ☐ You are maintaining a constant, alert lookout for obstructions, including traffic and debris.
- ☐ Lines aboard are neatly coiled out of the way.
- ☐ You know where the nearest harbor is in case you need a harbor in a hurry.
- ☐ You are keeping an eye on the weather, watching especially for sudden storms—summer squalls are like that—on the hori-

zon. Too, you tune in a marine weather forecast now and then.

☐ You are monitoring the distress frequency on the radiotelephone (2182 kHz or 156.8 MHz).

☐ There is more than enough fuel to get where you are going.

☐ You are checking the chart and watching buoys to see that you stay in the channels.

☐ Refuse is being placed in a container aboard.

☐ There is not too much water in the bilge (take a look) and no gasoline odor (sniff).

☐ Okay, break out the soda pop.

And finally, at the day's end, we employ a return checklist:

And home again

☐ You have pumped out the bilge water before docking.

☐ The fenders are in place while you slowly slip through the harbor, gauging current, wind, and sea.

☐ Mooring lines are ready—their inboard ends are secured to the appropriate boat cleats and their remaining lengths are neatly coiled and knot-free.

☐ The boat hook is handy to fend off if necessary.

☐ You are approaching the slip (or mooring) slowly, into the wind or current, whichever is stronger, if possible.

☐ The boat is secure at her slip (or mooring).

☐ Now, and not before, you switch off the engine.

☐ The children and the nonswimming adults wear preservers while they help clean the boat or romp about dockside.

☐ All perishable food is being removed.

☐ Refuse has been disposed of ashore.

☐ You warn the kids to put their preservers back on.

☐ The boat is being hosed down with fresh water. If you feel up to it (or can persuade someone else to do it) you will scrub-brush the hull (whatever its material) with a detergent and then hose it clean. Wooden hulls, and particularly wooden hulls in salt water, need this treatment more than fiberglass hulls do.

☐ The outboard motor (or the lower unit of the stern-drive) is swiveled clear of the water.

☐ You holler at the kids for not wearing their preservers and insist they be put on.

☐ All switches, windows, hatches, and doors are closed.

☐ The cockpit canvas is snapped on.

☐ You have double-checked to see that all mooring lines are secure.

☐ The boat keys and registration certificate are in your pocket.

☐ On the way home you tactfully tell your guests to wear boating shoes next time.

Special handling situations

It it possible to get into some "tight" boating situations despite your skill and care. Completely submerged objects near the surface and uncharted shoals are the most common culprits. Although on the whole each is a rare event, it obviously pays to be able to cope with them.

If your boat hits something beneath the water—at slow speeds you will hear a thud; at high speeds you will feel the thud—take your engine out of gear immediately and set the anchor; or, if you are in open and deep water, allow the boat to drift. Inspect the bilge for damage. If water in the bilge appears to be rising look for the leak. The automatic bilge pump, of course, will go on by itself. If you have only a manual pump, now is the time to use it. Have the people aboard take brief turns pumping while you attempt to plug the leak.

If you can get at the source of water from inside the hull you can half the flow, or at least slow it, with some kind of jury patch: first cover the break with a flat piece of pliable material like a square of canvas, seat cushion, bunk mattress, foul-weather jacket—look around; and then lay down a rigid backstop

One of the best ways to attract attention when you need help is with a flare, and one of the best flare kits is this one from Olin, which for around $60 includes day and night flares and an International Orange distress flag.

like a breadboard or a chunk of plywood. You may be able to wedge this piece in place by driving a nail or screw over the board and into a frame nearby.

You may be able to rig a patch on the outside of the hull, which is generally preferable since the water pressure will help to hold it in place. A piece of canvas and a couple of nails should hold until you make port and have the boat hauled.

If your inspection of the bilge uncovers no leak, start the engine and proceed slowly. You want to discover now if the propeller or the shaft on which it turns has been damaged. If the boat begins to vibrate, some damage has occurred. If the vibration is slight, head for port slowly. To avoid extensive damage if the vibration is severe, do not run the engine. Anchor and wait for a tow. If you have a radiotelephone you can inform the Coast Guard that you are disabled; they will come for you (no charge, but you boat will probably be inspected and if it is not up to par you may be cited, which may mean a fine). Probably, however, you can get some passing boat to tow you in. Recognized distress signals include:

Raising and lowering your outstretched arms (stand where you can be seen).

Continually sounding your horn.

Repeatedly firing a gun (unless doing so violates local law).

Using various flares, especially smoke flares during the day. Unofficial distress signals, which usually work, include:

Screaming "Hey!" at the top of your voice.

Flying a flag upside down.

Having everyone aboard wave "Come here" to a passing boat. The best bet is to try them all if necessary (your local U. S. Coast Guard District Office should have a free sixteen-page booklet called *A Pocket Guide for Visual Distress Signals*-CG-152). Once some boatman learns you need help, almost without exception help will come willingly and promptly. When you get the opportunity, return the courtesy.

Should you run aground while you are traveling at high speed, follow the same procedure for discovering and, if necessary, temporarily repairing any leaks as it outlined above. If it happens while you are traveling at a slow or moderate speed—and there is reason enough to be traveling at slow or moderate speeds in waters with which you are unfamiliar—put the engine into reverse immediately. You may be able to slip back into deep water. If this does not work, try shifting your passengers, first, forward in order to free the propeller and, then, if you cannot power-free, aft if it is the bow that is aground.

Suppose you are still stuck.

Relax.

Have a beer.

Smoke if you feel like it.

If you are grounded in sand, switch off the engine so that the cooling system does not clog. Look over the situation. Where is the deep water? Is it low or high tide? Are there any boats around that can toss a line to you and tow you off? Can you set an anchor out in deep water—throw it out, row it out, or swim it out—and then haul the boat free by sweating in on the anchor line?

If everything else fails, put out a call for non-emergency help on the radiotelephone or start sending visual distress signals. So you'll be a little late.

There are many times, of course, when the situation requires immediate action, as when your boat is sinking in deep water and away from any apparent help. This is the classic "mayday" (from the French *m'aidez,* "help me") condition, and if you have a radiotelephone this is the time to use it. Learn the emergency procedure now and learn it cold:

Before you get under way it's a good idea routinely to run down a checklist like the one published on page 85.

On 2182 kHz if your radiotelephone is equipped with MF band, or 156.8 MHz (channel 16) if it is equipped with VHF band, say:

"Mayday! Mayday! Mayday!

"This is (identify your boat, your location and the nature of the emergency, and tail off with)

"Over."

In identifying your boat, give its name, call sign, length, type, colors, and whatever else distinguishes the craft. For location, do the best you can; if you know latitude and longitude, by all means provide those data, but if you don't, "twenty minutes south of ____________" or "about ten miles out from ____________ ____________" (or whatever) will do. When communication conditions are poor, use the following phonetics to spell difficult words.

A ALPHA
B BRAVO
C CHARLIE
D DELTA
E ECHO

F FOXTROT
G GOLF
H HOTEL
I INDIA
J JULIET
K KILO
L LIMA
M MIKE
N NOVEMBER
O OSCAR
P PAPA
Q QUEBEC
R ROMEO
S SIERRA
T TANGO
U UNIFORM
V VICTOR
W WHISKEY
X X-RAY
Y YANKEE
Z ZULU

MERCURY

Chapter 9
A KNOT OR TWO

Cars you park; boats you make fast. Of the thousands of knots man has invented (see *Ashley Book of Knots,* for example), only whaleboatmen and Eagle Scouts can manage more than a small fraction. Stay calm. Boatmen, I have found, can get by with *one* knot—the bowline (rhymes with stolen)—though a few more in the repertoire are expedient. I have seen sailors whiz through these knots with one hand and in half a gale. It is awesome, considering that it still takes me several tries to square a square knot. Repetition is the key. And one of these days I am going to master the square knot.

How they are done

Handiest of the knots, the bowline is probably the most difficult of those presented here, but worth the fuss. Besides its versatility—use it whenever an "eye" (loop) is needed—it neither slips nor jams.

The clove hitch (page 92), simply two loops with an end tucked under, secures the boat to a piling or similar structure for a short stay. Adding a couple of half hitches, as shown, will provide a more permanent hookup. Or use a bowline instead.

Bowline.

Simple to make (some say), the square, or reef, knot (page 92) has many applications for light-duty work, most common of which is to join two light lines. Put under strain, the knot tends to jam, raising havoc when you want to undo it.

Cleating (page 92), when finished, is a figure 8 with one loop reversed and is the correct way to make a line fast to a cleat. Start by

Left: Clove hitch. Right: Half hitches.

Square, or reef, knot.

taking a turn around the cleat's "far side," the side opposite the strain (step A). Steps B and C take you from there. Note in Step C that by snubbing the free end back under, you can release the knot without disturbing the boat. Most boatmen take a half dozen figure 8's before "locking" with the reverse; one or two will do.

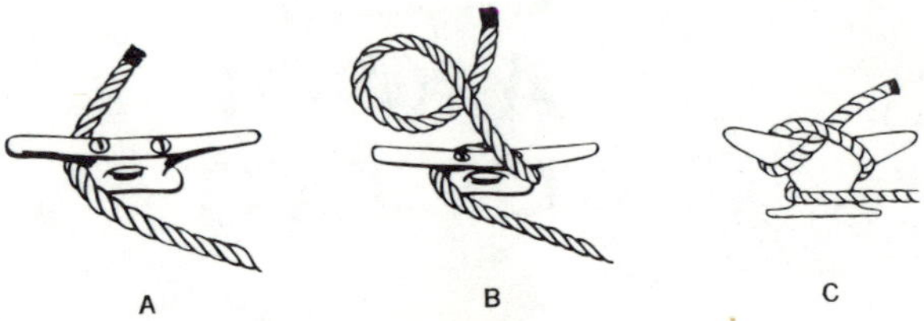

Cleating.

Chapter 10
READING THE NAUTICAL ROAD SIGNS

The buoy (rhymes with fooey) is to the boatman what the traffic sign is to the motorist; it helps you to determine where you are and what you should do next. It is the principal element in the aids-to-navigation system maintained by the Coast Guard. Other common markers that make up the over-all "aids" system are the various beacons you'll find especially to help at night and in other conditions of poor visibility. You ought not to attempt your first cruise without knowing the basics about each of these.

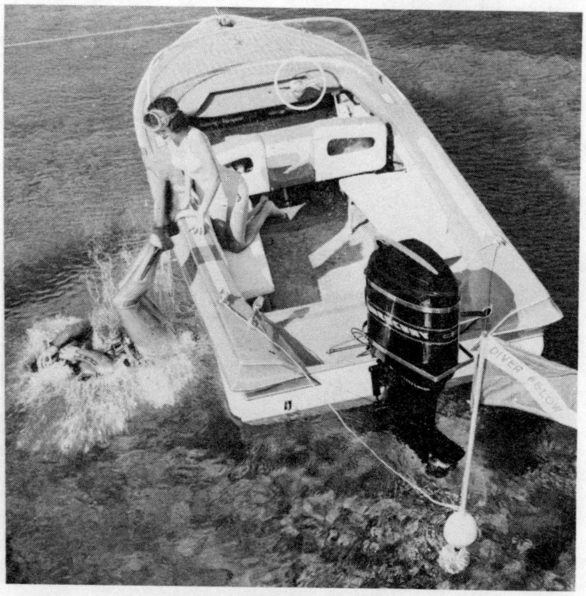

There are some 25,000 buoys under the Coast Guard's jurisdiction. There are who-knows-how-many private markers, such as the one shown here to indicate a diver is in the waters. If the meaning of a marker is unclear, slow down and proceed with caution.

Buoys

There are some 25,000 buoys on waters over which the Coast Guard has jurisdiction. Most numerous are the unlighted can and nun buoys, distinguished by their shape and color. Cans are cylindrical and generally black, nuns are conical and generally red. The color tells you on which side the marker should be

A help in remembering on which side you should pass a channel buoy is the phrase "red-right-returning"—keep the red buoys to your starboard (right) side when returning from the sea or from a larger body of water into a smaller one.

Banded buoys, whether can or nun shaped, denote their significance by the color of the uppermost band. If red, as here, treat it as a nun; if black, as a can.

passed. When returning from the sea, or from some large body of water to a smaller one, you keep the red buoys to your starboard—just remember "red, right, returning"—and black buoys to port. Most of these buoys are numbered or lettered or both, with the unlighted black cans always having odd numbers and the unlighted red nuns, even ones.

If the can or nun is banded black and red, it's a channel junction or channel obstruction buoy and it's the color of the *top* band that tells you which side to pass: if it's black, treat it as a can; if it's red, treat it as a nun.

A black and white vertically striped buoy, either a can or a nun, simply marks the mid-channel.

Steer clear of wreck buoys (they have the letters "WR" on them) and yellow buoys (they mark quarantine anchorage areas).

White buoys designate official anchorage areas.

All these buoys, as well as other markers discussed below, are located on your official charts with, all things considered, almost pinpoint precision. Unlighted can "13," just to choose a random example, will be shown by a solid black diamond over a black dot with the legend C "13" next to it. Thus by plotting a buoy-to-buoy course on a chart you can follow it at sea, and conversely by spotting markers at sea you can locate them—and so, you—on the chart.

All the abbreviations and symbols used on National Ocean Survey charts are explained in a booklet entitled "Chart No. 1" and sold ($1.50) by NOS, Distribution Division, C44, Riverdale, Md. 20840. Get it, by all means.

To help you navigate at night, certain of these buoys carry lights. Their color and characteristics help you to identify the marker.

If the color of the light is *green,* you're looking at a can buoy and so it is designating the left-hand side of the channel as you return from seaward, or a junction or obstruction in the channel if the marker is a red-and-black-banded buoy whose uppermost band is black.

If the color is *red,* you're looking at a nun buoy and so it is designating the right-hand side of the channel as you return from seaward or, again, a junction or obstruction in the channel if the marker is a red-and-black-banded buoy whose uppermost band is red.

If the color of the light is *white,* you're looking at a marker that may be on either side of the channel and is being used instead of a red or green light because greater visibility is desired. Seeing a white light, therefore, doesn't give you much information about the purpose of the buoy, but its phasing characteristics will.

If it is a *flashing light,* which means it is blinking on and off at a rate of no more than thirty times per minute, you are looking at a can, nun, or special-purpose buoy. Count and time the flashes, check the color of the light, and then locate that buoy on your chart.

If it is a *quick flashing light,* which means no fewer than sixty blinks per minute, take

Light beacons come in all sizes and shapes. Their light characteristics and significance can be learned from the appropriate chart.

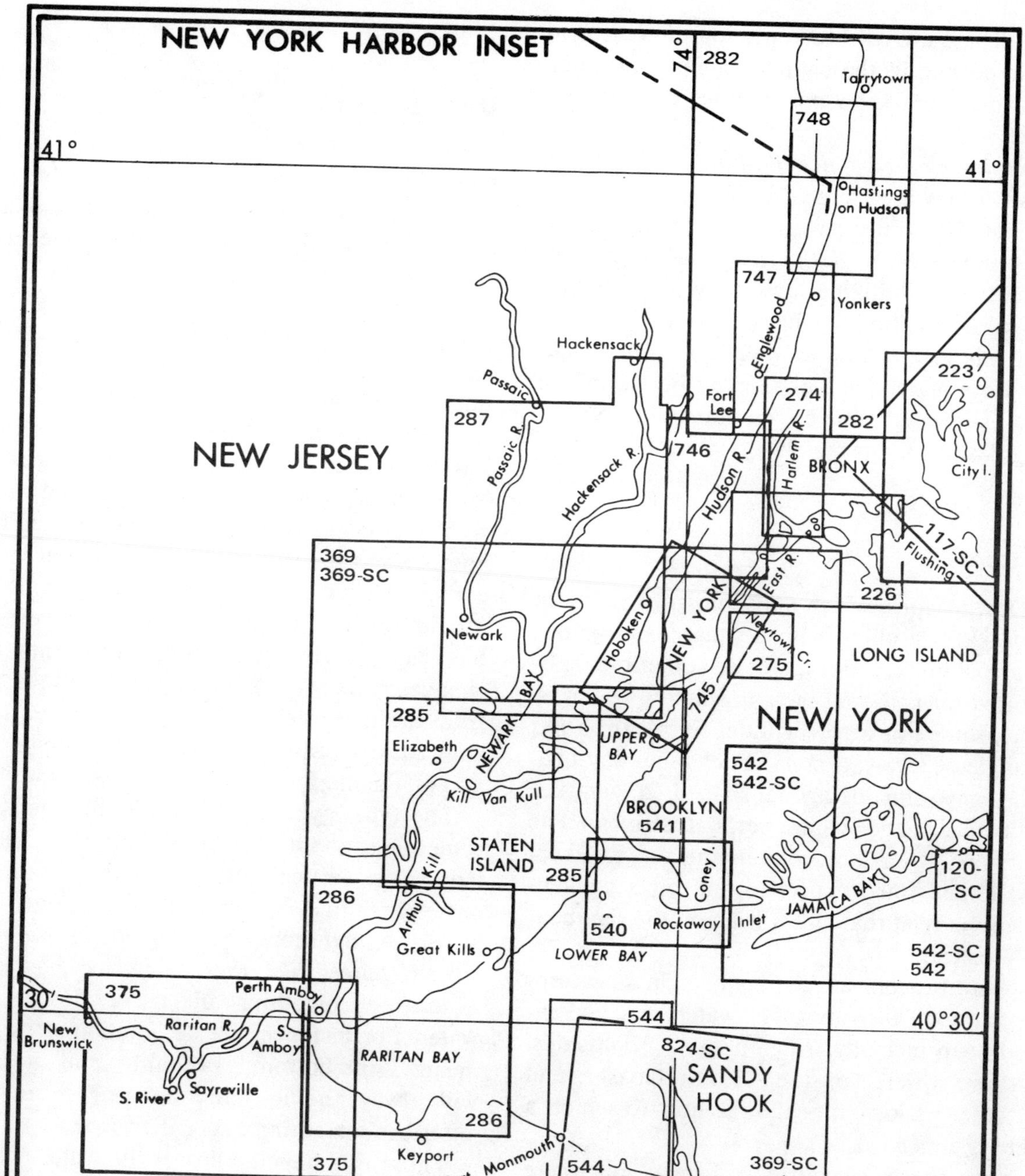

Small portion of National Ocean Survey Nautical Chart Catalog 1, the brochure from which you figure out which charts you need.

care! These are used to warn you of some dramatic change in the channel, such as a quick turn, or to mark an obstruction. Check your chart.

An *interrupted quick flashing light,* which means it has a pattern of blinking at a rate of at least sixty times per minute, stopping for a fixed time (that's the interruption), and then resuming the blinking again, always indicates a channel junction or obstruction buoy.

If it is a *short flash followed by a long flash,* it is on a midchannel or fairway buoy, and so it can be passed close by, on either side. Short-long flashing lights are always white.

Beacons

Day beacons, which may consist of no more than a single piling with a square, triangular, or arrow marker at its top, are sometimes substituted for cans and nuns in shallow water. A black square or arrow will denote a can; a red triangle or arrow, a nun. Midchannel day beacons have an octagonal-shaped daymarker with black and white vertical stripes. The numbers, letters, or combination of numbers and letters you'd expect to find on a conventional buoy at that site will be on the day beacon instead.

Night beacons are the major light structures on or along the navigable waterways and include, principally, lighthouses, lightships, offshore towers (on the Atlantic Coast), and all other major nautical structures to which a light is appended.

Your charts, of course, will show you where these night beacons are located, the distance and direction from which they can be seen when visibility is good, their individual characteristics, and why they are there. Considerably more detailed information about each of these beacons is found in the Coast Guard books entitled *List of Lights and Other Marine Aids,* which everyone calls the *"Light Lists"* (see page 104). It's wise to have them aboard for use with the charts.

Using a chart

Like most boatmen, I'd guess, I have spent many hours studying charts for no other reason than that they are fascinating. Water depths, or soundings, location of channels and navigation markers, dumping areas and artillery areas, old wrecks and new wrecks, harbors, marinas, underwater pilings—all this and more is given, as I have said, with remarkable accuracy on official cruising charts.

Sources for these charts are listed in the following chapter. You'll note that the prices are low enough to enable you to replace old charts with the latest ones; you'll find the edition number and date of revision in the lower left corner of each chart, as a rule. Revisions are usually made annually, or every two years at the most. Between editions you can add changes from your personal observations and from the free weekly *Notice to Mariners* (ask your local Coast Guard District office to put you on the mailing list).

The type styles used on the chart tell you something about the item being described. Roman, or vertical, letters, like these, describe something that remains dry even at high water. A lighthouse, for example. *Italic or slanted letters like these,* describe bodies of water, or something under or floating on water. For instance, the designation *sft,* which means "soft bottom," probably mud or sand, will always be in italic lettering because it describes something under the water.

Those tiny fingers all over the water area of the chart indicate the depths there, at low water for tidal regions, in feet, especially in shallow areas, or in fathoms (there are 6 feet to a fathom); on a few of the newest charts, depths are given in meters (there are 3.28 feet to a meter) and decimeters (.1 of a meter). The greater the number of soundings given, the bumpier is the bottom, which means marked irregularity in the depths of water. The flatter the bottom the more uniform are the depths, and therefore fewer soundings will appear on the chart.

Basins and channels that have been dredged are delineated on the charts by a pair of broken lines indicating width and course. Controlling depth will be given somewhere within those broken lines, or very near by. "Controlling depth" means that nowhere in the dredged area is the depth less than *x* feet, but bear in mind that the information is accurate only as of the date of dredging. I have gone aground right in the middle of a channel in Chesapeake Bay (among other places). When you're cruising areas that are notoriously shoal with frequently shifting bottoms, and Chesapeake Bay is such a place, proceed slowly and keep an eye on what the local boats are doing. Cardinal rule: don't rely entirely on what the local boats are doing; they likely know the waters well enough to squeeze through a slot with a foot of water on each side.

Land features are included on charts only to the extent that they are considered useful to the boatman: towers, large buildings, tanks, stacks, that sort of thing, that are near or alongside the shoreline. The shoreline is shown by a solid line if it has been surveyed or a single broken line if it has not; the location given is for high water, and on most large-scale charts a dotted line indicates low-water location. Contour lines, which indicate land areas of equal height, give you some idea of what the topography is like ashore—flat, hilly, or mountainous.

You can see why poring over nautical charts is fascinating. And why it is essential you have the right charts for the waters you plan to cruise.

(*Photo by Frank Rohr.*)

Chapter 11
CRUISING

Pleasures are personal; how you find them is your business. Certainly your boat provides potential: you can fish, race, harbor-hop, or picnic, among the possibilities (see Chapter 12). Probably, though, cruising will take priority—new waters, new landfalls, new friends, a sweet sense of accomplishment when your destination heaves into sight. Planning leads to cruising success, but avoid executing the plans with such rigidity as to rob the cruise of its color. Invite your crew to participate in the preparation, taking care to invite no more than your boat can accommodate comfortably. She may *hold* twenty but *accommodate* six. Consider compatibility, too. Quarters are tight. Relationships become intense and, if shaky, shattered.

Decide now where you want to wind up each day, having multiplied the hours you want to run daily by your boat's average *cruising* speed. List ports to put into en route. Fuel stops and food stops. Rest stops and overnight stops. Choose alternatives. Chart these courses. Cushion the schedule so that waiting out a squall does not entirely upset your timing. Then change whatever and whenever your fancy feels.

Jot down the things you have and the things you need, tracking your inventory by checking off items as you go along. Finally, just before you leave but while you are aboard, double-check. The accompanying checklist will help to insure that nothing essential or desirable is left behind. It is based on the assumption that your boat is already equipped with what law (Chapter 6), and logic (Chapter 7) require. You have only to tailor it to *your* needs, *your* pleasures.

Where to get help

Dry as crust or vividly readable, cruising guides abound, some available for the asking, some for bare production costs. Rely with discretion on the information they provide, keeping in mind the necessarily temporary nature of such guides, impeccably correct, perhaps, at the time of publication. Use them to picture and to anticipate the conditions you

Your cruising checklist

check	double-check	
☐	☐	alarm clock
☐	☐	asbestos pot holders
☐	☐	ashtrays
☐	☐	bathing suits
☐	☐	batteries (spare)
☐	☐	bedding
☐	☐	belts
☐	☐	Bermudas
☐	☐	beverages
☐	☐	bilge cleaner
☐	☐	blouses
☐	☐	boarding ladder
☐	☐	boat cleaning materials
☐	☐	books, magazines
☐	☐	buckets
☐	☐	bulbs (spare)
☐	☐	bug spray
☐	☐	cameras, film
☐	☐	can opener
☐	☐	charts, charting tools
☐	☐	checkbook
☐	☐	cigarettes, lighter
☐	☐	citizenship proof
☐	☐	coats
☐	☐	copper pads
☐	☐	corkscrew
☐	☐	cosmetics
☐	☐	credit cards
☐	☐	cruising guides
☐	☐	cuff links
☐	☐	dinghy
☐	☐	dipstick (spare)
☐	☐	ditty bags
☐	☐	diving gear
☐	☐	dresses
☐	☐	drugs (special)
☐	☐	dungarees
☐	☐	engine parts (spare)
☐	☐	eyeglasses
☐	☐	fans
☐	☐	fill-pipe "keys" (extra)
☐	☐	first-aid kit
☐	☐	fishing tackle
☐	☐	flashlight
☐	☐	food
☐	☐	fresh water
☐	☐	fuel (reserve)
☐	☐	fuses (spare)
☐	☐	galleyware
☐	☐	games, toys
☐	☐	garbage bags
☐	☐	gloves
☐	☐	hair care items
☐	☐	handkerchiefs
☐	☐	hangers (wood or plastic)
☐	☐	hats
☐	☐	heaters
☐	☐	horn (extra)
☐	☐	ice
☐	☐	ignition keys (extra)
☐	☐	insurance coverage
☐	☐	jackets
☐	☐	laundry bag, detergent
☐	☐	lighter fluid, flint
☐	☐	lines (extra)
☐	☐	lock permit
☐	☐	logbook
☐	☐	manuals
☐	☐	matches
☐	☐	money, traveler's checks
☐	☐	motor scooter
☐	☐	musical instruments
☐	☐	nail clipper, file
☐	☐	nail polish, remover
☐	☐	napkins
☐	☐	ovenware
☐	☐	pajamas
☐	☐	paper cups, dishes
☐	☐	paper toweling
☐	☐	penknife
☐	☐	pens, pencils, pads
☐	☐	phonograph, records
☐	☐	plastic bags
☐	☐	playing cards
☐	☐	pocketbooks
☐	☐	portable TV
☐	☐	radio
☐	☐	rags
☐	☐	raincoats
☐	☐	registration papers
☐	☐	robes
☐	☐	scissors
☐	☐	sealant
☐	☐	sewing kit
☐	☐	shaving needs
☐	☐	sheath knife
☐	☐	shirts
☐	☐	shoehorn, laces, polish
☐	☐	shoes
☐	☐	shorts
☐	☐	shower cap
☐	☐	silverware
☐	☐	slacks
☐	☐	slippers
☐	☐	soap
☐	☐	socks, stockings
☐	☐	spices
☐	☐	sponges
☐	☐	stamps
☐	☐	stationery
☐	☐	stove fuel
☐	☐	string
☐	☐	suits
☐	☐	sunglasses
☐	☐	suntan lotion
☐	☐	sweaters
☐	☐	tape recorder, tapes
☐	☐	telephone numbers
☐	☐	tide tables
☐	☐	ties
☐	☐	tissues
☐	☐	toilet paper
☐	☐	tools (extra)
☐	☐	toothbrushes, paste
☐	☐	towels
☐	☐	travel iron
☐	☐	underwear
☐	☐	vacuum cleaner
☐	☐	vacuum jug
☐	☐	wallet
☐	☐	washcloths
☐	☐	watches
☐	☐	water skiing gear
☐	☐	weathercast schedules

will encounter—the charm, the romance, the sudden shoals, the harbors you can swing in to, the marinas that stud the shores. Sources of state boating information are included in the listing below so that you can learn what is demanded by local boating regulations.

Cruising aids you can send for

Charts

U. S. Coastal Waters: Besides the Atlantic, Pacific, and Gulf coasts, such bodies of water as the Hudson River and the Intracoastal Waterway are included in the charts sold by Distribution Division, C44, National Ocean Survey, 6501 Lafayette Ave., Riverdale, Md. 20840. Its SC (small craft) series is geared for pleasure-boat use. Write for free Chart Catalogs (specify whether you want the Atlantic and Gulf coasts, the Pacific Coast, or Alaska) to determine which charts you need. Prices: $3.25 for conventional charts, $3.50 for small-craft charts in folio form, $2 for small-craft charts in pocket-fold form.

Great Lakes: Coverage also includes Lake Champlain, the New York State Barge Canal system, and a portion of the Minnesota-Ontario Border Lakes. Available from the Lake Survey Center, 630 Federal Bldg., Detroit, Mich. 48226. Catalog free.

Mississippi River and tributaries: For charts of the Mississippi north of the Ohio River, write to U. S. Army Engineer District, 536 S. Clark St., Chicago, Ill. 60605. For the portion below the Ohio, write to Mississippi River Commission, P.O. Box 80, Vicksburg, Miss. 39181. Chart catalog and *Mississippi River Navigation* booklet free.

Missouri River and tributaries: Charts are handled by U. S. Army Engineer District, 6012 U. S. Post Office and Court House, Omaha, Neb. 68102. Ask for free listing.

Ohio River and tributaries: Charts for the waterways between Pittsburgh, Pa., and the Mississippi are sold by the U. S. Army Engineer District, P.O. Box 1159, Cincinnati, Ohio 45201.

Tennessee and Cumberland Rivers: Write to U. S. Army Engineer District, P.O. Box 1070, Nashville, Tenn. 37202. Supplemental source for the Tennessee is the Tennessee Valley Authority, Maps and Engineering Records Section, 102A Union Bldg., Knoxville, Tenn. 37901.

Canadian Waters: Write to Hydrographic Chart Distribution, Department of the Environment, Room 230, 615 Booth St., Ottawa, Canada. Ask for free *Coastal and Inland Waters* catalog. Other cruising publications of interest that concern Canadian waters are:

Cruising Georgian Bay (aerial maps, lists of port services and facilities), available from Belhaven House, 12 Dyas Rd., Don Mills, Ontario. *Cruising the North Channel* (covers area between Manitoulin Island and north shore of Lake Huron), available from Belhaven House.

Yachtsman's Guide to the Great Lakes (besides the Great Lakes, waterways covered in remarkable detail include the St. Lawrence and the Richelieu rivers), available from Seaport Publishing Co., 843 Delray Ave., S.E., Grand Rapids, Mich. 49506. *Coast Pilots* for Canadian waters are available from Hydrographic Chart Distribution, Department of the Environment, Room 230, 615 Booth St., Ottawa, Ontario, Canada.

Foreign Waters: Published by the Defense Mapping Agency Hydrographic Center, Washington, D.C. 20390. General catalog and ten regional catalogs are available free.

Miscellaneous

Coast Pilots: Hard-cover books that supplement coastal and intracoastal charts with incredibly detailed descriptions of courses, distances, depths, locations of yacht clubs and repair facilities, tides, currents, and much more. The eight volumes sell for $6 each. Available from the Distribution Division, C44, National Ocean Survey, Riverdale, Md. 20840. For those waters covered by the Lake Survey Center (see under *Charts* above) the corresponding book is the *Great Lakes Pilot,* sold ($8) also by the Lake Survey Center, 630 Federal Bldg., Detroit, Mich. 48226.

Light Lists: Descriptions and locations of federal aids to navigation including lighthouses, radio beacons, and lighted and unlighted buoys. Volume I ($4.75) spans the Atlantic Coast from the St. Croix River, Me., to Little River, S.C.; Volume II ($4.60), from Little River to Texas' Rio Grande, plus the Antilles; Volume III ($3.15) covers the Pacific Coast and islands; Volume IV ($2.30), the Great Lakes; and Volume V ($3.15), the Mississippi River system. Available from Superintendent of Documents, U. S. Government Printing Office, Washington, D.C. 20402.

Notice to Mariners: Free weekly pamphlet published by the Defense Mapping Agency Hydrographic Center, Washington, D.C. 20390, to keep mariners current on changes affecting U.S. waterways, enabling boatmen to correct their charts. "Local Notices" are published by Coast Guard District offices; ask to be put on the free mailing list.

Tide Tables, Current Tables, Tidal Current Charts: Each is a publication of the Distribution Division, C44, National Ocean Survey, Riverdale, Md. 20840. The *Tables* are $3.75 each, the *Current Charts,* $4 each.

Handbook of Boating Laws: Thorough wrap up of state and federal boating laws in four editions ($1.95 each) for southern, northeastern, north-central, and western states. Write to Outboard Boating Club of America, 401 N. Michigan Ave., Chicago, Ill. 60601. Ask for membership details, too, incidentally, if you belong to a boating club; free OBC-member services include newsletters, tailored suggestions for organization and boating activity, and bulletins on pertinent governmental actions.

Weather Guides: In the event you're more into weather than simply tuning to a local forecast, you'll be interested in the following: *The Hurricane,* an illustrated 22-page booklet published by the National Oceanic & Atmospheric Administration and available from the Superintendent of Documents, Washington, D.C. 20402; and *Weather Forecasting,* an illustrated 40-page booklet from the same sources as the foregoing publication.

Guides: Several major oil refining companies offer free cruising services, including quite useful booklets and charts showing the locations of marinas selling their products. By using these guides to transfer marina sites to your cruising charts, you can pinpoint your potential fuel stops when planning your cruise. Write to: Esso Touring Service, 15 W. 51st St., New York, N.Y. 10019; Gulf Tourguide Bureau, P.O. Box 8056, Philadelphia, Pa.; Mobil Touring Service, 150 E. 42nd St., New York, N.Y., 10017; and Texaco Waterways Service, 135 E. 42nd St., New York, N.Y. 10017.

Boating agencies

State Boating Agencies

Alabama: Department of Conservation, Water

Safety Division, State Administration Bldg., Montgomery, Ala. 36104.

Alaska: Department of National Resources, 344 Sixth Ave., Anchorage, Alaska 99501. Boat registration handled by Coast Guard.

Arizona: Game and Fish Department, 2211 W. Greenway Rd., Phoenix, Ariz. 85023.

Arkansas: Game & Fish Commission, State Capitol Grounds, Little Rock, Ark. 72201.

California: Department of Harbors and Watercraft, 1416 Ninth St., Sacramento, Calif. 95814.

Colorado: Game, Fish & Parks Department, 6060 Broadway, Denver, Colo. 80216.

Connecticut: Boating Safety Commission, Department of Agriculture and Natural Resources, State Office Bldg., Hartford, Conn. 06115.

Delaware: Small Boat Safety Division, Commission of Shell Fisheries, P.O. Box 512, Lewes, Del. 19958.

District of Columbia: Metropolitan Police Department, Harbor Precinct, 550 Maine Ave., S.W., Washington, D.C. 20024. Boat registration handled by Coast Guard.

Florida: State Board of Conservation, 107 W. Gaines St., Tallahassee, Fla. 32304.

Georgia: State Game and Fish Commission, Trinity-Washington Bldg., Atlanta, Ga. 30334.

Hawaii: Harbors Division, Department of Transportation, Pier 11, Honolulu, Hawaii 96809.

Idaho: Motor Vehicle Division, Department of Law Enforcement, P.O. Box 34, Boise, Ida. 83707.

Illinois: Conservation Department, Boat Licensing Division, 400 S. Spring St., Springfield, Ill. 62706.

Indiana: Department of Natural Resources, 605 State Office Bldg., Indianapolis, Ind. 46209.

Iowa: State Conservation Commission, State Office Bldg., 300 Fourth St., Des Moines, Iowa 50319.

Kansas: Forestry, Fish and Game Commission, P.O. Box 1028, Pratt, Kan. 67124.

Kentucky: Department of Public Safety, Division of Boating, New State Office Bldg., Frankfort, Ky. 40601.

Louisiana: Wild Life and Fisheries Commission, 400 Royal St., New Orleans, La. 70130.

Maine: Bureau of Watercraft Registration and Safety, State Office Bldg., Augusta, Me. 04330.

Maryland: Boating and Recreation Division, Department of Chesapeake Bay Affairs, State Office Bldg., Annapolis, Md. 21404.

Massachusetts: Division of Motorboats, 100 Nashua St., Boston, Mass. 02114.

Michigan: Department of State, 2100 N. Larch St., Lansing, Mich. 48906.

Minnesota: Department of Conservation, Boat and Water Safety Division, 625 N. Robert St., St. Paul, Minn. 55101.

Mississippi: Boat and Water Safety Commission, Suite 240, 720 President St., Jackson, Miss. 39202.

Missouri: State Commission, P.O. Box 603, Jefferson City, Mo. 65101.

Montana: State Board of Equalization, Capitol Bldg., Helena, Mont. 59601. For boat regulations, State Fish and Game Department, Water and Hunter Safety Section, Helena, Mont. 59601.

Nebraska: State Game, Forestation and Parks Commission, Lincoln, Neb. 68509.

Nevada: Fish and Game Commission, P.O. Box 10678, Reno, Nev. 89501.

New Hampshire: For boat registration, write to Division of Motor Vehicles, Department of Safety, 85 London Rd., Concord, N.H. 03301. Powerboats operating on state waters must register with the state; on U.S. navigable waters within the territorial limits of New Hampshire, with the Coast Guard.

New Jersey: Department of Conservation and

Economic Development, Bureau of Navigation, Box 1889, Trenton, N.J. 08625.

New Mexico: State Park and Recreation Commission, P.O. Box 1147, Santa Fe, N.M. 87501.

New York: Division of Motorboats, State Conservation Department, N.Y. State Campus, 1220 Washington Ave., Albany, N.Y. 12226.

North Carolina: Motorboat Section, Wildlife Resources Commission, Box 2919, Raleigh, N.C. 27602.

North Dakota: State Game and Fish Department, Bismarck, N.D. 58501.

Ohio: Department of Natural Resources, Watercraft Division, 1952 Belcher Dr., Columbus, Ohio 43224.

Oklahoma: Boat and Water Safety Division, Room 500, Will Rogers Bldg., State Capitol, Oklahoma City, Okla. 73105. For registration, State Tax Commission, 2101 N. Lincoln Blvd., Oklahoma City, Okla. 73105.

Oregon: State Marine Board, State Agriculture Bldg., 635 Capitol St., N.E., Salem, Ore. 97310.

Pennsylvania: Fish Commission, South Office Bldg., Harrisburg, Pa. 17127. For registration, Miscellaneous License Division, Pennsylvania Department of Revenue, Harrisburg, Pa. 17127.

Rhode Island: Registry of Motor Vehicles, Executive Department, State Capitol Bldg., Providence, R.I. 02903.

South Carolina: Wildlife Resources Department, Division of Boating, P.O. Box 167, Columbia, S.C. 29202.

South Dakota: Department of Game, Fish and Parks, State Office Bldg., Pierre, S.D. 57501.

Tennessee: Tennessee Game and Fish Commission, 706 Church St., Doctors Bldg., Nashville, Tenn. 37203.

Texas: Highway Department, Motor Vehicle Division, 40th and Jackson, Austin, Tex. 78703. For a free listing of public launching ramps, write to Texas Parks and Wildlife Department, John H. Reagan Bldg., Austin, Tex. 78701.

Utah: Boating Division, State Park and Recreation Commission, 132 S. 2nd W., Salt Lake City, Utah 84101.

Vermont: Department of Public Safety, Marine Division, Montpelier, Vt. 05602.

Virginia: Game and Inland Fisheries Commission, P.O. Box 1642, Richmond, Va. 23213.

Washington: Washington State Parks and Recreation Commission, P.O. Box 1128, Olympia, Wash. 98501. Boat registration handled by Coast Guard.

West Virginia: Department of Natural Resources, Boat Licensing Section, State Office Bldg., Charleston, W. Va. 25305.

Wisconsin: Wisconsin Conservation Department, P.O. Box 450, Madison, Wis. 53701.

Wyoming: Game and Fish Commission, P.O. Box 1589, Cheyenne, Wyo. 82001.

Territorial boating agencies

Puerto Rico: Marine Operations Department, Port Authority, San Juan, P.R. Registration handled by U. S. Coast Guard in San Juan.

Virgin Islands: Department of Commerce, Marine and Aviation Services, Charlotte Amalie, St. Thomas, Virgin Islands.

Federal boating agencies

Coast Guard: Recreational Boating Safety Division, U. S. Coast Guard Headquarters, Washington, D.C.

Local Coast Guard

First District, 150 Causeway St., Boston, Mass. 02114.

Second District, Federal Office Bldg., 1520 Market St., St. Louis, Mo. 63103.

Where the Coast Guard Districts are.

Third District, Governors Island, New York, N.Y. 10004.

Fifth District, Federal Bldg., 431 Crawford St., Portsmouth, Va. 23705.

Seventh District, Room 1018, Federal Bldg., 51 S.W. First Ave., Miami, Fla. 33130.

Eighth District, Customhouse, New Orleans, La. 70130.

Ninth District, 1240 East Ninth St., Cleveland, Ohio 44199.

Eleventh District, Heartwell Bldg., 19 Pine Ave., Long Beach, Calif. 90802.

Twelfth District, 903 U. S. Appraisers Bldg., 630 Sansome St., San Francisco, Calif. 94126.

Thirteenth District, 618 Second Ave., Seattle, Wash. 98104.

Fourteenth District, 677 Ala Moana Blvd., Honolulu, Hawaii 96813.

Seventeenth District, P.O. Box 3-5000, Juneau, Alaska 99801.

Canadian provinces—regional sources of cruising information

Alberta: Alberta Government Travel Bureau, 331 Highways Bldg., Edmonton, Alta.

British Columbia: Government Travel Bureau, Department of Recreation and Conservation, Victoria, B.C. For the location of "marine parks," send for the free *British Columbia Marine Parks* folder from Parks Branch, Department of Recreation and Conservation, Parliament Bldgs., Victoria, B.C., Canada.

Manitoba: Travel and Publicity Branch, 500 Norquay Bldg., Winnipeg, Man.

New Brunswick: Travel Bureau, P.O. Box 1030, Fredericton, N.B.

Newfoundland: Newfoundland Tourist Development Office, Confederation Bldg., St. Johns, Nfld.

Nova Scotia: Nova Scotia Travel Bureau, Provincial Bldg., Halifax, N.S.

Ontario: Department of Travel and Publicity, Toronto, Ont.

Prince Edward Island: Travel Bureau, P.O. Box 1087, Great George St., Charlottetown, P.E.I.

Quebec: Provincial Publicity Bureau, Government Bldg., Que.

Saskatchewan: Travel Bureau, 1819 Cornwall St., Regina, Sask.

Yukon Territory: Department of Travel and Publicity, Box 939, Whitehorse, Y.T.

An inland cruise

The cruising tale that follows has been adapted, by permission of *Motor Boating* magazine. I have two reasons for including this cruise here. One is that, from the planning stage on, I was skipper and so am able to tell in detail what went into the cruise. These comments appear in italics, interspersed throughout the original text. The other reason is that these waters, as exciting and lovely as any I have explored, can be negotiated with agreeable ease so that the readers who are shy on cruising experience might well consider cutting a similar course.

Champlain is a tall, deep body of water, interrupted here and there by low-lying islands, particularly in its upper reaches. [*Unless you are closely hugging the shore or rounding a point too tightly you will be cruising in water two to three hundred feet deep, free from concern about running aground and from having to stick to the channels. Lakemen say Champlain is pure enough to draw upon for your drinking supply, but I wouldn't count on it; it is clean enough, in any case, to relieve the helmsman from having constantly to skirt debris, and that is a rare asset on most waterways today.*] The lake flows north, spilling into Canada's Richelieu River. As you cruise down the lake, which means up toward Canada, New York's Adirondacks trail alongside to port. To starboard in summer, stands of rock maple carpet Vermont's Green Mountains. Along the shore, red cedar and pitch pine cast long shadows out onto the waters.

Together with two Frenchmen, sixty Indians, and twenty-four birch-bark canoes Samuel de Champlain came to these waters July 4, 1609. We arrived 354 years later, four strong, aboard a 35-foot cruiser whose inventory of gear and cheer were beyond Sammy's rashest dreams. [*"We" were Eileen (my wife) and I and, for a part of the trip, Marge and Dale Phillips. Dale is an art director for a paperback publisher, Marge, his wife. When they left, Dr. and Mrs. Henry Spector, friends of ours, boarded for the balance of the voyage. Our gear aboard fairly squared with the "cruising checklist" that appears earlier in this chapter. We had used this list in our preparations and—no kidding—this became one of the few times that nothing we would have liked along had been left behind. The cheer we carried was an ample inventory of beer and booze, in labels catering to everyone's taste. Be sure to control the liquor locker with discretion: drunken driving is as illegal and reckless afloat as it is ashore.*] Where the explorer slithered about to avoid hostile Iroquois, we splashed and stretched, waving recklessly to whoever would look our way. Where some of America's fiercest battles once were waged as the colonies girded for independence, we split the waters at a reasonably steady 2,600 rpm, a red-balled sun skidding off the blue of our hull. We had come to Lake Champlain.

Three and a half days before, departing Lindenhurst, N.Y., and swinging around Long Island's southern shore to the Hudson River, we had begun to make our way north at a leisurely pace, soon to traverse the locks that open into Champlain Canal. [*The first is a federal lock at Troy, N.Y., the last, Lock 12, at Whitehall, N.Y. The permit necessary to use these locks is available free from the Su-*

perintendent of Operation and Maintenance, State Department of Public Works, State Office Bldg., Albany, N.Y. Allow at least a couple of weeks from the time you mail in a completed form (available from the same source) for your permit to come. In a pinch, however (I'll hear about this), you can get a permit in minutes at the first lock you come to; just act innocent about the whole business. Locks make navigation possible over what would otherwise be waterfalls, raising or lowering the boat from one level to another. After hitching a line to a cleat aboard and passing it around the far side of one of the bollards (these look like fat fire hydrants) along the top edge of the lock, you maintain control over the boat, while the water level changes, by taking in or paying out the free end of the line.] On the afternoon of the fourth day our boat was secure in Point Bay Marina, Charlotte, Vt., and we were taxiing to nearby Shelburne Country Inn for roast beef—rare and butter soft. [*Generally someone in the marina office can get a taxi to you within a half hour at most, which, for the men aboard, is plenty of time to hose down the boat and switch into shoreside clothes. If there are women aboard, better let them change into their shoregoing clothes before calling for a taxi. To keep expenses down, we used a motor scooter to make short hops to supermarkets for supplies now and then. Ours was a Valmobile, particularly compact because it folds into a neat seat. While we cruised, the scooter was lashed in the cockpit, and despite being drenched by occasional seas that broke over the quarter, it never failed to start after a little urging.*]

There is a great variety of harbors the boatman can visit, setting his own pace and his own course; almost anywhere he points he will come to deep water. The order is unimportant since it is possible to run the length of the lake —about 110 miles—in a day aboard any modern cruiser, the navigation made simple by such prominent markers as The Four Brothers, South Hero, Valcour, and Cumberland Head. [*Except for Cumberland, which is a singularly large point jutting out from the New York shoreline, these are all distinctive islands. By studying the charts often*

Lock walls are grimy, and so, to save your hull's appearances, wrap your fenders with disposable burlap, build a "fenderboard," which is a long plank with fenders secured behind it, and hang it over the side, or do whatever else comes to mind. Here, while the boat descends, Henry Spector pays out line and Ann Spector uses the boat hook to maintain a safe distance. (*Photo by the author.*)

Simultaneously, Eileen Penzer tended the chores aft, paying out line and fending off with a second boat hook. We were cruising on a 35-foot sedan cruiser and found that four—I was at the helm—were just right to handle the locking procedures easily. Eileen's perched atop a fold-up motor scooter that proved handy for picking up groceries, finding a taxi at different landings, and serving as an extra cockpit seat. (*Photo by the author.*)

Marinas come in all shapes and styles, with only one thing in common: permanent berths are hard to come by. This one is in Plattsburgh, New York. (*Photo by the author.*)

and memorizing such landmarks before you cruise new waters, you will be able to pick out your position with ease when the time comes. The Four Brothers, for example, are the only such grouping of islands on the Lake and so are unmistakable when spotted.] It is the sunnier side of prudence to keep a nearby harbor in mind as you cruise along, for when the wind rips out of the north or south, seas on the lake build short and steep, making conditions uncomfortable for the most able of boats and hazardous for lesser vessels.

But mostly Champlain is calm and, as Puget or Long Island Sound boat populations go, virtually abandoned. Even in the thick of a summer's day [*we were there in mid-August*] yours will be almost the only vessel slicing the stillness. Ashore it is wide, green unbroken country, a land of maple syrup poured carelessly over Harrington sausage on mornings trimmed with mist or closed with fog. It is a land of back dirt roads and slim streams, of wild honeybees, mink and partridge, of buried arrowheads and marble quarries, of cellars bulging with bottles, homemade nails, a rusting musket, old lanterns, chain, saws, a broken anchor, blue and white earthenware, wood, preserves, wagon gear, and a fiddle or two. Its citizens are Green Mountain Boys still, who build their own fences and bottle their own cider, who organized the nation's first professional basketball team, discovered laughing gas, invented the steam calliope, and have four licensed fortune tellers. Put aside as many days as you can to explore the land and meet its people.

Compared with, say, Florida's Fort Lauderdale, boating facilities along either Champlain shore are sparse. Still, as a study of your chart should prove, you can plan your food, fuel and overnight stops to accommodate nearly any day's run you like. [*Although our over-all direction for the first half of the cruise trended north, each day's specific course on the lake wasn't drawn until the night before; that way we were flexible enough to account for bad weather and to concentrate as much time as we could spare in places we were particularly enjoying. In planning courses I multiply the cruising speed of my boat by the amount of cruising time I am willing to put in daily, and if the answer is close to the distance of a destination being considered, then that's it, I plan to go. If there is a marked discrepancy between the distance and the allotted cruising time, I simply choose another destination for the day's run, closer to my first choice and as attractive as possible. To find these destinations, I select likely-looking harbors from the charts, see what various cruising guides have to say about them* (*see page 103*) *and, if I still draw a blank, contact local marinas and chambers of commerce for advice. Regardless of how fast the boat I am cruising in is capable of going, incidentally, I clamp her cruising speed to about 20 mph, and less, of course, if she is a slow boat. Then if the water is nastier than I had expected I will still be running close to schedule; if conditions are calm we all can doubly enjoy the day's run, really getting to see not only what there is where we are going but what there was where we have been. Usually I allot about seven hours a day for cruising, shoving off about nine in the morning and winding up about four in the afternoon. It is true that the waters are calmest and at their most majestic dress at early dawn, around sunrise, but it has been many years since I have been able to get up at sunrise. Putting in at a marina or dropping anchor in a quiet cove at about four in the afternoon leaves enough daylight to put the boat in order, prepare dinner, and go for a swim.*] Two outstanding Vermont-side marinas are the Point Bay Marina at Charlotte (phone: 825-2431) and the Shelburne Marina at Shelburne Point (phone: UN 4-5786); over on the New York side consider the Marine Base at Essex (phone: 963-7700). The Vermont shore is rich with comfortable motels, among the coziest of which is Shore Acres overlooking the lake at North Hero Island. The irregular coastlines of both shores and most of the islands yield an abundance of coves in which you can swing the night at anchor, but in early summer stock up on insect repellent, for green flies and hungry mosquitoes will find you out. In August, however, the insects are gone and the black night skies are sequined with stars —low, close, brilliant. [*I find that a nice arrangement is to spend three consecutive nights aboard and the fourth at a motel or hotel. Although many marinas offer coin-operated washers and dryers for the use of visiting boatmen, many prefer to accumulate the laundry and have it done for them overnight when they stay ashore. The "three on, one off" plan fits right into this laundry scheme.*]

Plan to spend some extra time, if you can, at the Shelburne Museum in Shelburne, Vt.; it is open from nine to five daily between May 25 and October 20. The museum cannot be done in a day. [*Sprawling over forty acres, the museum is to New England what Williamsburg is to America, an exciting, enriching collection of authentic Americana. Boatmen will be particularly interested in the displays of stern boards and figureheads, and in the Ticonderoga exhibit, the best existing example of American-built sidewheelers.*] A few miles north of Shelburne is the town of Burlington, where from atop a bluff at Battery Park the view across Champlain is magnificent. It is about 50 miles east from Burlington to the highest Green Mountain peak, Mount Mansfield (4,393 feet), a favorite of skiers in the winter but hardly less lovely in summer dress. The Stowe chair-lift on Mansfield operates daily from June 22 to Columbus Day. Side trips such as these, to the museum or to Mansfield, make welcome diversions from daily boating fare.

Except that your time will dissolve in attempting to exhaust the historic locales along Champlain's shores, it is tempting to cruise farther north, right into Canada. After clearing with Customs on the Richelieu River, a colorful stopping point is the small, French-speaking town of St.-Jean, about 20 miles up from the international boundary. [*There is a dramatic change as you leave Champlain and enter the Richelieu. The former is open, expansive, and bordered by rolling terrain; the latter is narrow, winding, and to each side the land is flat for as far as you can see. Each has its own fascination. Because the river is shallow—a foot or two in places—its dredged channel is well buoyed, in places so closely that you feel you are running between picket fences. Soon after you cross the boundary going north, a large sign on one of the bridges you pass under directs you into Canadian Customs at Ash Island; this will be on your starboard side. After securing alongside the wharf here, you walk into a small wooden building, answer a few questions, perhaps be asked to show a birth certificate or a voter's registration card to establish your citizenship, receive a cruising permit, and be back on your way—all in twenty minutes or so. On the return leg you must clear with U. S. Customs. To do this you can put in at Rouses Point Marina, on your starboard side slightly south of the international boundary, where one of the marinamen will telephone a Customs man to drive in from town to clear you. At a minimum the officer will ask what you are bringing from Canada; he may inspect your boat to see for himself. It took us about an hour to clear here.*]) The St.-Jean's Yacht Club offers slips, fuel, power, and repair service. [*A reference to "power" when one speaks of marina services means there are electrical outlets near the slip into which you can plug those home-type conveniences you've brought along—razor, toaster, television set, etc.—or, if your boat has an auxiliary home-type wiring system, as more and more cruisers do, you can activate it by plugging a master connection from the boat into the dockside outlet. Everything you do to avoid draining your boat's batteries is a plus for safety. When buying fuel in Canada, incidentally, bear in mind that the gallon you are getting is an Imperial one, 20 per cent greater than the gallon to which U.S. boatmen are accustomed.*] Buses in St.-Jean run to Montreal, about an hour's journey if traffic is not too heavy.

For your Richelieu navigation you will want Canadian Hydrographic Chart 1326, published by the Department of Mines and Technical Surveys, Ottawa, Canada. Chart 1325 takes you farther north to Sorel and the St. Lawrence Seaway.

For your Champlain cruising you will want Lake Survey Charts 171–174; these can be ordered (4 charts, $1 each) from the U. S. Army Engineer District, Lake Survey Department, 630 Federal Bldg., Detroit, Mich. 48226. A chart catalog is free from the engineers. Prices have increased now, and newer charts are available. Check the free catalogs of both the Lake Survey Center, 630 Federal Bldg., Detroit, Mich. 48226, and the National Ocean Survey, Distribution Division, C44, 6501 Lafayette Ave., Riverdale, Md. 20840. [*As I usually do, I ordered charts I knew I would need and others I might need if some side trip should tempt us. I got them about three months before the departure date, which gave me plenty of time to pencil in some principal compass courses to the lake, pinpoint fuel stops (transferred to my cruising charts from free Gulf, Mobil, and Texaco cruising guides), and generally discover what to expect. Eileen helped in all this planning and, with my encouragement, added stops that she wanted to make. Like St.-Jean, so we could bus to Montreal where the shops are.*]

Even in midsummer take blankets along to contend with the cool Champlain nights. Leave room in the refrigerator for Vermont corn and apple cider, sold at shoreside stands and stores along the lake. And of course remember your camera.

Chapter 12
BESIDES CRUISING, WHAT?

Whether cruising occupies most of your boating time or not, you will want to do other things with your boat. Here are examples of the more popular activities.

Boat camping: If your boat lacks sleeping, cooking, or sanitary facilities, or if, in any event you have an affinity for tenting out, consider boat camping. Sleeping and cooking are done ashore with, if you choose areas reserved for camping, toilet facilities nearby. A request to the appropriate state agency—usually the department of conservation—should bring a listing of such shoreside campsites; too, check any of the *Recreational Vehicle Camping Guides* now sold at most newsstands.

Diving: There is an invitingly weird and challenging kingdom beneath your hull, often incredibly beautiful. Besides simply sightseeing, diving permits easy boat-bottom maintenance, spearfishing, and hunting for sunken treasure (known wrecks are located on official boating charts). Underwater gear ranges from uncomplicated face mask and flippers to elaborate self-contained underwater breathing devices. Dealers in diving gear usually sponsor diving clubs.

Fishing: So pleasant is angling, Izaak Walton observed, that like virtue it is a reward to itself. Rare is the boat without an assort-

Boat camping lets you range farther afloat in a small boat. Collapsible tents can be stowed aboard for each day's run.

Scuba diving for fish or fun is exciting sport, at least if it is in warm, clear waters. Diver's flag, which is a white diagonal on a red background, warns approaching boats to keep away.

Both relaxing and exciting, fishing is perhaps the one activity every boatman indulges in, whatever size his craft. Financing the sport can be kept to pennies (dropline and hook) or substantial sums (fighting chairs, outriggers, tuna towers, etc.). (*Photo by Frederic Maura. Bahamas News Bureau.*)

Check your charts to find a beach you can nose up to for a picnic lunch. Remember to keep an eye on the tide to avoid being stranded.

Gunk-holing is the art of poking into out-of-the-way places, a sport especially suitable for the small boat.

ment of drop lines aboard. More commonly, gear includes a half dozen rods and reels, a plethora of hooks, lures, swivels, and sinkers, a gaff or two, and a net. The sportfisherman (Chapter 1), of course, has much more. Check state sources (Chapter 11) to determine local fishing regulations on fresh water.

Gunk-holing: A small boat and a vigorous curiosity are all you need to gunk-hole—to poke into the countless untrammeled dips of the shoreline and discover perhaps the chance remnants of times and seas long gone or perhaps simply a stretch of solitude, no less. It is an activity for the adventurer who is willing to go slowly enough to see what is otherwise overlooked. It is to travel far in Concord, as Thoreau has put it.

Predicted logging: Not speed but knowledge—of currents, winds, and your cruiser—is what counts here. You predict how long it will take you to cruise between three or more designated points. The man who comes closest wins. Simple? Sure, except that timepieces and speedometers are barred on the run. Besides eliminating the hazard of speed, logging sharpens the skipper's skill. For details write Cruiser Division, American Power Boat Association, 22811 Greater Mack, St. Clair Shores, Mich. 48080.

Racing: Whatever the boat, there is a racing class for her. Emphasis is on matched starts, speed, and handling, usually with more glory than money at stake. Courses run from inland circuits of a few miles or so to long-distance, bone-shattering ocean grinds. The most influential racing organization in the United States is the American Power Boat Association, 22811 Greater Mack, St. Clair Shores, Mich. 48080.

Trailering: Small-boat trailers, generally for craft to 21 feet or so, open boating vistas to any captain with a yen to roam. Public launching ramps dot the waterways in growing numbers. De luxe trailers, plushly padded and fitted with push-button winches, make trailering a joy. Models should conform to your boat's contours, weight, and length. Check with the state sources listed in Chapter 11 to learn launching ramp locations and local

Skill, stamina, and courage are among the human requisites for speedboat racing. Organized competition goes on throughout the year, largely under the aegis of the American Power Boat Association. (*Photo by Roland Rose. Bahamas Ministry of Tourism.*)

By trailering you can greatly extend your boating horizons. Write to the state boating agencies listed in Chapter 11 to find out where the public launching ramps are located.

Water skiing continues to be a popular pastime, keeping the kids entertained and the women (obviously) trim.

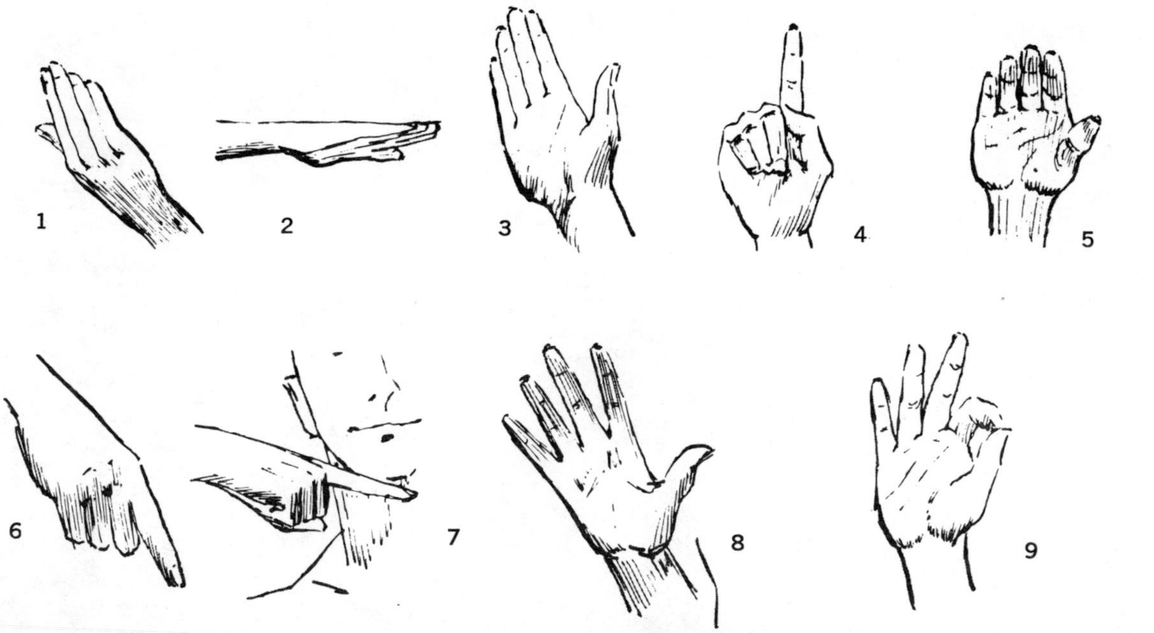

The American Water Ski Association has developed the hand signals above for communication between boat and skier. 1. Speed up—open palm up with arm sweeping upward. 2. Slow down—open palm down, with arm extended and sweeping downward. 3. Turn—with open palm, describe curve with hand in direction desired. 4. Whip off—point to direction and give quick circular motions with extended finger. 5. Jump—with open palm, signify soaring motion by sweeping hand forward and up. 6. Back to dock—with arm straight, bring extended forefinger sharply downward, or point downward with elbow bent. 7. Cut motor—move extended finger across throat with cutting motion. 8. Stop—raise hand with fingers outstretched. 9. Everything okay—the traditional signal: "O" made with finger and thumb.

trailer laws. Too, ask your local branch of the American Automobile Association for a copy of its *Trailer Pointers and Driving Hints* booklet.

Water-skiing: This is an inexpensive sport to equip for and master. You will need skis, a towline with handle, and a ski belt. The boat should be capable of logging at least 18 mph when towing. Many states require an observer in the boat and prohibit skiing between dusk and dawn (check state sources in Chapter 11). The largest water skiing organization is the American Water Ski Association, P.O. Box 191, Winter Haven, Fla. 33880.

Wood, fiberglass, or metal, hulls occasionally need to be painted, seasonally if it's wood, and when the hull appears to need it if it's anything else. Choose a good grade marine paint, and only a marine paint, made for your hull's material. (*Photo by the author.*)

Chapter 13
TENDER LOVING CARE

Many authorities—most, I think—invoke the salty cliché *shipshape and Bristol fashion* as the standard of boat maintenance. The real boatman, they say, keeps every inch of his vessel in perfect, not just good, condition. Maybe. If so, there are remarkably few real boatmen. Between the tinkerer who would rather care for his craft than use her and the antitinkerer who avoids all work however camouflaged fall most boatmen. They do the work tenderly, lovingly, carefully—but not with such passion as to make driving a screw preferable to driving the boat. The well-heeled can have their boat maintenance done for them, losing neither muscle nor time in the process. For most of us of more moderate fortune, maintenance is a matter of compromise. Do what is necessary, and then go boating.

Well, what is necessary? That which is needed to make the boat seaworthy. If time and money and energy hold out, fine, do more. If not, forget it.

Seaworthiness in part is the ability of the boat to contend with the waters in which she is used, come what may. A rotted plank will not stand much battering. A burned-out running light may cause a collision. "Mayday" (the international distress signal) sent on a radiotelephone that does not work will bring no help. Weed-clogged intakes may stall the engine at a perilous time. These examples indicate the kind of attention that is called for to produce seaworthiness, as distinguished from fluff. Making chrome gleam besides making it clean is fluff. Sanding each hull coating so thoroughly that the next coat lies down like a mirror is fluff. Matching wood stain with exquisite precision is fluff. I do not say these effects are not desirable. Of course they are. But I for one would rather be boating.

More how to do it

There is nothing terribly difficult about competently maintaining a boat. By starting with an understanding of just what it is you want to achieve, the problem is more a matter of how to do it than what to do. And how-to-do-it advice abounds. Even good advice. Brochures, booklets, and personal answers to individual

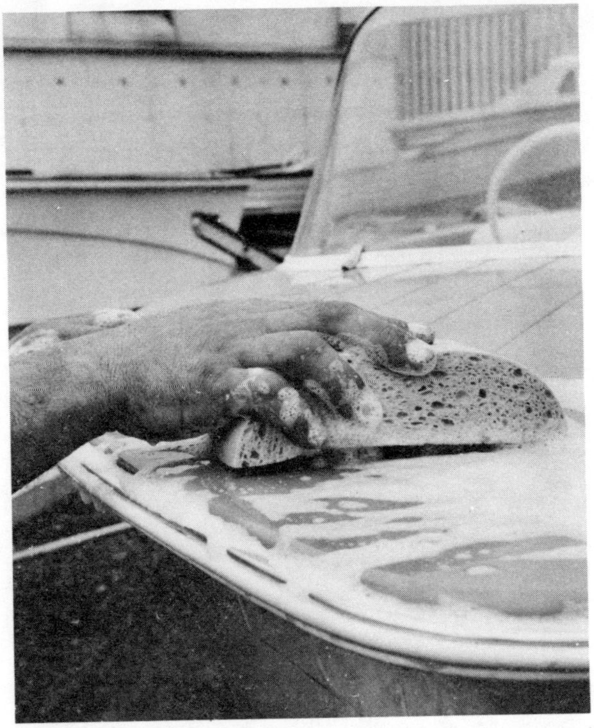

On fiberglass boats, scrubbing down the hull will keep up appearances; on wooden hulls, of which there are fewer and fewer, cleaning is critical, and the more so in salt waters.

problems can be had for the cost of a letter to any manufacturer of a product apt to be used in the work—paints, varnishes, hardware, and so on. Boating magazines annually devote an issue or two to the best techniques of spring fitting-out (commonly the March or April issue) and fall hauling-out (October or November issue). Boat-maintenance books flourish. Boatyard employees, unless the yard's policy is to do all the work itself, often provide good counsel. Marine dealers and boating organizations are still other productive sources. (The major boating trade organization in the United States is the National Association of Engine and Boat Manufacturers, 666 Third Ave., New York, N.Y. 10017.) Steer clear of amateur advice, as you do when boat buying (Chapter 2).

Here are the basic boat-care guidelines that are applicable to all boats.

Prepare an organized plan to cover before-you-launch and after-you-haul (respectively spring and fall in northern regions) boat maintenance. Prudently, many skippers add a thorough midseason check to this.

Do as many chores as are practicable after hauling the boat in order to get afloat sooner come launching time.

Invite those persons who use the boat to help in her care, assigning specific chores to each. Kids, incidentally, thrive on bottom painting—the boat's and theirs.

Resist the lure of cheap materials and tools. The cost of frequent replacement is greater than the apparent savings.

You can adopt the general scheme that follows to prepare a maintenance plan for your boat, trimming or expanding it in spots, of course, to match your needs.

Before you launch

Clean the hull exterior, using a mild detergent, a scrub brush, and plenty of fresh water. On fiberglass hulls try a cleanser that has no abrasive ingredient, to avoid dulling the gel coat. I've found Fantastic, for example, to be effective except around the waterline, which tends to get the grimiest. There, a paste cleaner for fiberglass—Seven Seas is one brand—will work, but test it on a small area first, rubbing lightly. If you missed removing some barnacles when you last hauled, scrape them off now with a putty knife. If you plan to paint (see below) be sure the hull is clean, free of grease and oil, sanded as necessary, and dry.

Any dry rot—it will look and feel spongy—in your wooden hull should be treated, either with some special product (one I have used successfully is Calignum) or by carving out the fungus-infected piece and replacing it. If the rot is extensive and you are not handy at woodworking, have a yard do the job. Treat it promptly, in any event, or the damage will spread.

Tighten all hull fastenings, replacing any that are bent, stripped, or corroded.

Fill any gouges in the hull with one of the many "surfacing" compounds your marine dealer sells; if the filling is to be done beneath the waterline, use a compound made for underwater application.

Paint and varnish as necessary. Regardless of the nature of your boat's hull material, use "antifouling" paint on its bottom (from the waterline down). This will discourage marine organisms (especially various kinds of worms) from attacking the hull and marine plant life from attaching itself to it, in this way avoiding both damage and loss in performance. If the hull is metal, apply a prime coat of an anticorrosive paint before applying the antifouling paint. Follow this procedure in both fresh and salt water. Above the waterline brush or spray on only a good-quality marine paint and varnish. A sensible painting order is to do the hull topsides (above the waterline) first, then the bottom, and, lastly, the waterline, or boat-topping, itself.

Clean and polish all metal fittings—rails, cleats, anchor brackets, and so forth. In salt water you should do this often (ideally at the end of each day's use) to prevent the metal from pitting.

Replace sacrificial zinc anodes. These are small, inexpensive (about $3), teardrop-shaped pieces of zinc alloy to be attached near or on underwater metals you want to protect from corrosion—the lower end of the outboard motor, for example, or the inboard engine's drive shaft, the rudders, a metal hull, etc. Because of its chemical properties, the zinc and not the metal you want to preserve will corrode; that is why it is called a "sacrificial" anode.

Run a hose over the deck to be sure no leaks have developed during the boat's layup. If you do get some dripping inside, recaulk suspected seams (Thiokol or silicon-based sealants make marvelous plugs).

Now is the time to thoroughly clean the cockpit, cabin, and lockers—before the season's supplies are brought aboard. Install the shelves you needed last year.

Examine all steering components, readjusting and replacing as necessary. Then lubricate all joints, springs, and function-bearing surfaces.

Slight nicks in the propeller can be filed smooth; if there is serious damage, have the propeller reconditioned or replaced.

Prepare the powerplant (explained below).

Bring on and stow equipment and supplies.

Close all bilge drain openings before you launch.

Readying the engine—outboards

Have an engine manual for reference. Each new motor is sold with such a manual. If yours is missing, write to the manufacturer for one; they are free.

Consider having a yard mechanic do all the work. My yard gets $50 to commission an 80-horsepower motor, and the price includes keeping the motor's starting battery on a trickle charge for the winter. Even if you have a yard do the work, however, know what is involved; there may be a time when you will have to do the work yourself.

Install new, properly gapped spark plugs. Your manual will specify both the correct plug type to use and the ideal gap setting.

Change the lubrication in the lower unit. On most models you will see two screw plugs on the vertical drive portion of the motor. The upper one is a "vent" plug, the lower a "drain." Remove both plugs, and the old lube will ooze out of the drain. Be patient and allow all the lube to seep out. Now refill by squeezing fresh lube into the *drain* (the lower opening) until the vent opening overflows. The lube is packaged in disposable toothpaste-type tubes, but larger, the nozzle of which properly fits the drain opening. The manual tells you which type of lube you should use and how often it should be changed.

Put a light coat of oil on the throttle linkage and the motor clamp screws.

Breaker points should be changed after a

couple of seasons' use or sooner if you are having ignition trouble.

Drain and clean the carburetor float bowl.

Drain and clean all fuel filters. If you do not have a fuel filter, get one and install it before you run the engine. Buy a type that can be cut into the fuel line between the tank and the motor. Filters sell for as little as $4, but be sure they are capable of removing water as well as dirt from the fuel. Ask the dealer.

Touch up any rusted or abraded spots on the motor exterior. Several companies make spray-can paints available in colors that match major motor brands.

After the boat is afloat you can tune the carburetor by adjusting the knobs marked "high speed" and "low speed" on some models. The manual will show you where they are, and whether it is advisable for you to fiddle with these settings. If not, it's a job for your dealer. If you can, first warm the engine well by cruising her at open throttle for about five minutes. Then, while still at open throttle and with someone at the helm, slowly turn the "high speed" knob (to the right or left, depending on results) until the engine runs both fast and smooth. Trial and error will get you there. Once you are satisfied with the high-speed performance, slow down and idle the motor. Then adjust the slow-speed knob until the motor runs smoothly. Before you jump to change the settings again during the season, be sure first that your fuel is clean and your spark plugs are in good shape. Keep a supply of spare plugs aboard.

Readying the engine—inboards and stern-drives

Have an engine manual for reference. Each new boat is sold with such a manual. If yours is missing write to the engine manufacturer for one; they are generally free.

After ascertaining the charge—this varies too much with individual yards and engines for me even to suggest an average—*consider having your yard mechanic do all the engine commissioning work.* If you do, however, know what is involved; as with outboards, there may be a time when you will have to do the work yourself.

Unless this is the engine's first season, in which case your dealer has probably already done what is necessary and you can skip this entire engine section for now, or unless you did this step when you last hauled, *change the oil* by pumping it out of the crankcase and replacing it with the grade recommended in your manual. Replace the cartridge in the oil filter.

Check the manual to learn what engine accessories need a few squirts of light oil or dabs of grease and where the oil or grease cups are. These parts include the generator, water pump, and distributor as a rule.

Inspect the cooling-system hoses, and if they are not in excellent condition—no cracks, worn spots, or kinks—replace them now. If they seem in excellent condition but have had a couple of seasons' use, replace them anyhow.

Remove and inspect the spark plugs. If the porcelain is crazed or the electrode appears foul, replace it. The manual specifies the plug type and gap setting to use. You can buy a spark plug gap gauge at an auto supply store for about $1. Most inboarders I know figure that plugs are cheap enough to replace each year as a matter of course. This is probably good advice for distributor breaker points and a condenser as well. Your manual tells you how to install these and then adjust ignition timing; methods vary with engine make.

Remove and clean the carburetor float bowl and all strainers in the fuel lines.

Examine the ignition wiring. If cracked, replace it. If old, replace it. If merely suspect, replace it. These are pennies we are talking about, compared with a season's trouble-free performance.

It is good practice to wipe down the engine with an oily rag, leaving a light coat of oil to prevent rust. Paint any spots on the engine where the old paint has peeled.

Make use of the motor manual to prepare the engine for the winter layup or to ready it before you launch. If you do not have a manual, write to the engine manufacturer for one, including the year and serial number of the engine, in your request.

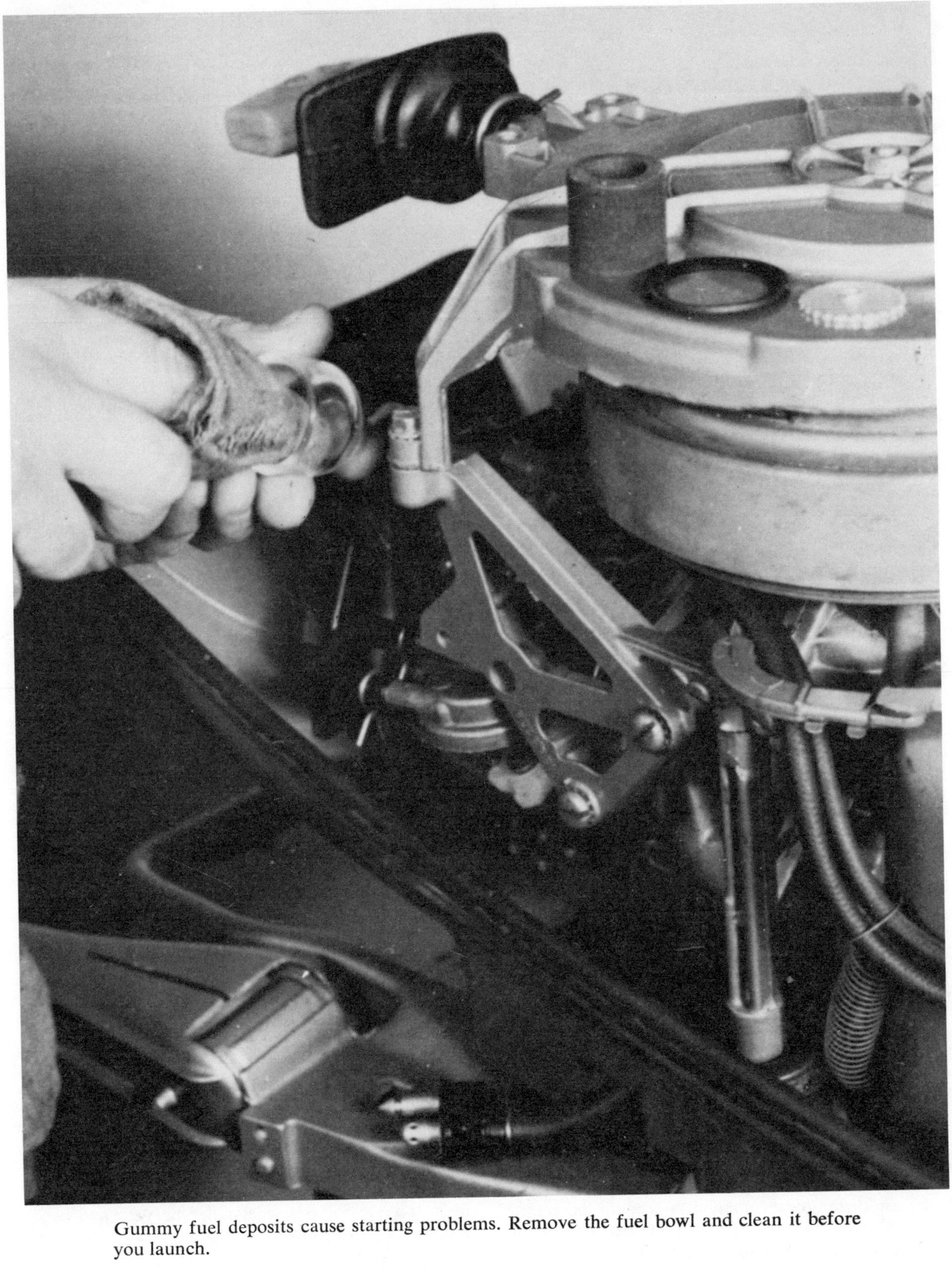

Gummy fuel deposits cause starting problems. Remove the fuel bowl and clean it before you launch.

If the starting batteries are in good condition—have the yard measure their output—*simply wirebrush the terminals and clamp on the cables.* Clamp them on, that is, if they are clean and not worn. Otherwise invest in new ones.

Tighten engine mounting bolts.

Install "screens" over the water intake fitting on the hull to filter foreign material.

If after launching the boat you find that the engine runs roughly at low or high speeds, a fuel mixture adjustment on the carburetor should correct matters. First warm up the engine and then turn the carburetor's "idle screw" (look in the manual for its location) until the engine beats smoothly. Avoid idling too far down or the engine will stall when you least want it to, while you are crawling into a dock, for instance. The high-speed adjustment calls for greater care in order to avoid producing too lean a mixture while you are tinkering; this can damage the engine. The safest procedure is to begin, with the throttle advanced, by having a clearly rich mixture: give the high-speed screw two full turns in the "rich" direction (it will be marked). Then slowly reverse the screw, toward "lean," until the engine speed decreases its revolution (check the tachometer for a drop in rpm). Then turn the screw back toward rich until the lost revolutions are regained.

During the season

Hose down the boat with fresh water after each day's use. If you do your boating in salt water, add a detergent once in a while to the clean-up routine.

Touch up paint and varnish as necessary. Choose days that are windless (so dust does not collect on the wet surface) and sunny (so the paint or varnish sets sooner) to do this work.

Change the inboard engine crankcase oil or outboard motor gearcase lubricant reasonably soon after reaching the hours of use specified in your engine manual. Generally this is 100 hours for the crankcase oil and 50 hours for the gearcase lubricant.

Take ashore those items that you stowed aboard before you launched, thinking they would be of use, that are not of use. That giant Stillson wrench, the double-boiler, a jar of garlic spread, long underwear . . .

Pour some liquid cleaner into the bilge about once a month; your neighboring boatmen will appreciate it.

Make a list of changes and repairs you want to make on the boat when you have time. Look at the list from time to time.

After you haul

Consider the chores you will have to do before you next launch, and do as many of them now as you can or as is practicable to do now. Of these, one worthwhile but often overlooked step is to put on a coat of bottom paint. Then, come spring, you need only roll on a second quick coating. In the meantime you will have helped your boat to weather the layup better by keeping the bottom from drying out. A coat of paint or varnish above the waterline helps too.

Open all doors and drawers, and upend all permanent-type mattressing (like the forward V-bunks with foam rubber cushions) for ventilation.

Clean and coat all chrome fittings with a polish or a petroleum jelly (I smear Vaseline on in the fall and wipe it off in the spring).

Take ashore everything you can store ashore. Afloat, a boat displaces its weight. Ashore, everything aboard becomes dead weight and puts a strain on the hull. Lighten the load as much as you can.

Either drain or fill the fuel tank. In no event should you leave it partially filled. It is not gasoline itself that is explosive but rather the mixture of gasoline fumes and oxygen, the product of a partially filled fuel tank.

Drain the head and work some disinfectant through a couple of times. Clorox does the job. Remember to empty the medicine locker.

Winterize the engine (explained below).

Rig a simple type of A-frame across the top of the boat so that your winter canvas will not sag when it rains or snows. Be sure you leave a drain in the bilge, incidentally, for rainwater to escape. Most boats have a screw-type fitting for this purpose. An alternative is to drill a ¼-inch hole through the lowest portion of the bilge. Just be sure to close the fitting or plug the hole before you launch. I scrawl a big note on the windshield with lipstick to remind me.

Put on a winter cover (most are canvas) and secure it snugly by running some lengths of line from one side of the cover to the other across the bottom of the boat. Ready-made covers come rigged with tie-lines and metal grommets. Ventilate the cover (a few slits about eight inches long with the edges stitched to prevent running will do) if it does not have built-in vents.

Pat the boat goodbye. (Tears.)

Winterizing the outboard

Consider having the yard do it while you work on the hull.

Remove the storage batteries and have the yard put them on a trickle charge for the layup period. Most boatyards are set up to do this.

By disconnecting the fuel line just before the boat is hauled and while the outboard motor is running, you will burn away what fuel is left in the motor's fuel lines. Just let the motor run itself out. Then try starting it a few more times. The fuel system should be clean now; just remove and clean the carburetor bowl and the fuel filter.

An adequate winter layup cover, vented, rigged over a sturdy frame, and tied down, will add years to your boat's life.

With the motor shroud (top cover) off, squirt some light oil on all the springs and movable joints you see. Then wipe the shroud and the lower unit with an oily rag. Some outboarders prefer to wax the painted surfaces.

If you change the gearcase lubricant now you will not have to do it in the spring.

Remove the spark plugs and squirt several drops of a rust-preventive oil into the openings. Turn the flywheel by hand and the oil will be distributed over the cylinder walls. Put back the plugs.

Winterizing the inboard and stern-drive

Consider having the yard do it while you work on the hull.

Change the oil now rather than after the layup so that acids that may have accumulated in the old oil do not damage metal parts. Many crankcases are fitted with a "hand hole" plate which can be removed. Remove this plate and wipe out what sludge may have collected at the bottom of the crankcase. If you do not have a hand hole plate on the crankcase you can remove the sludge with "flushing oil."

If your engine is fresh-water cooled (it has a closed recirculating cooling system which is probably better but is more expensive than salt-water cooling systems) *put in antifreeze in northern climates.* If it is salt-water cooled, flush the water jackets with fresh water for about twenty minutes. This can be done by disconnecting the water intake hose and putting it in a bucket of fresh water kept supplied by a running hose. Then open all the drain cocks on the engine block and accessories (check their location in the engine manual). When the system is empty, close the drain cocks and run the engine for a few minutes without water. The heat will dry the jackets. And finally, fill with antifreeze.

Coat internal working parts with oil. One popular way to achieve this is to feed engine oil into the carburetor air intake until the engine chokes and stalls.

Remove the spark plugs and pour a half cup of engine oil into each cylinder. Put back the plugs.

Touch up the engine exterior with paint where it is required.

All that's needed

Responsibility for maintenance, as for seamanship, is fixed upon the skipper. Both are continuing jobs, not ending with yesterday's courtesy, last week's repair, or the pages of this book. Besides acquiring fundamental boating skills, however, a fair measure of reason and conscientiousness are the only hurdles between you and a lot of boating pleasure.

Chapter 14
TALK ABOUT BOATING

"A yacht that cannot face an ocean breeze," said the New York *Times* on October 9, 1873, "or even an ocean gale is little better than a toy. . . . The main use and recommendation of yachting, next to its service in the improvement of marine architecture . . . the one thing that saves it from the stigma of an expensive idleness, is the hardihood, vigor, and contempt of danger that it naturally breeds."

The unnamed writer, of course, was speaking about yachting as it was then, a sprinkling of palatially gilded hundred-footers, driven by steam or canvas and owned by a handful of exceedingly wealthy sportsmen. Except for a relic here and there, or a notable exception to the production of today's pleasure boats, such yachts no longer exist. Perhaps such yachtsmen are gone as well. What remains, however, is some of their tradition, borrowed by them from the steamers and clipper ships of their time, and the square-riggers and whalers that preceded them. It manifests itself in much of the language that boatmen use or that a certain faction of oldtimers insist be used. "Port" (this was once *larboard*) and "starboard" (from *steerboard,* the side on which the rudder was located) for *left* and *right;* "beam" for *width;* "galley" for *kitchen;* "head" for *bathroom;* and so on. The etymology of each, when it can be learned, unfolds a fascinating tale. But how functional is the word? How necessary to continue its use, to avoid using, instead, terms of more common understanding?

The reader will have observed that throughout this book I have parenthetically defined strict boating terms with a word or phrase drawn from everyday speech. Since it is possible to do this, one may properly ask, why not simply discard the former? In part, this *is* being done despite the forceful objections of those who hold that what is old, what is traditional, is by that fact alone preferable to what is new. They slow the change but they do not stop it. Those words upon which the greatest number of persons agree at any given time are the "correct" terms simply because, whatever a dictionary or a purist or a traditionalist rules, they are the words that are being used.

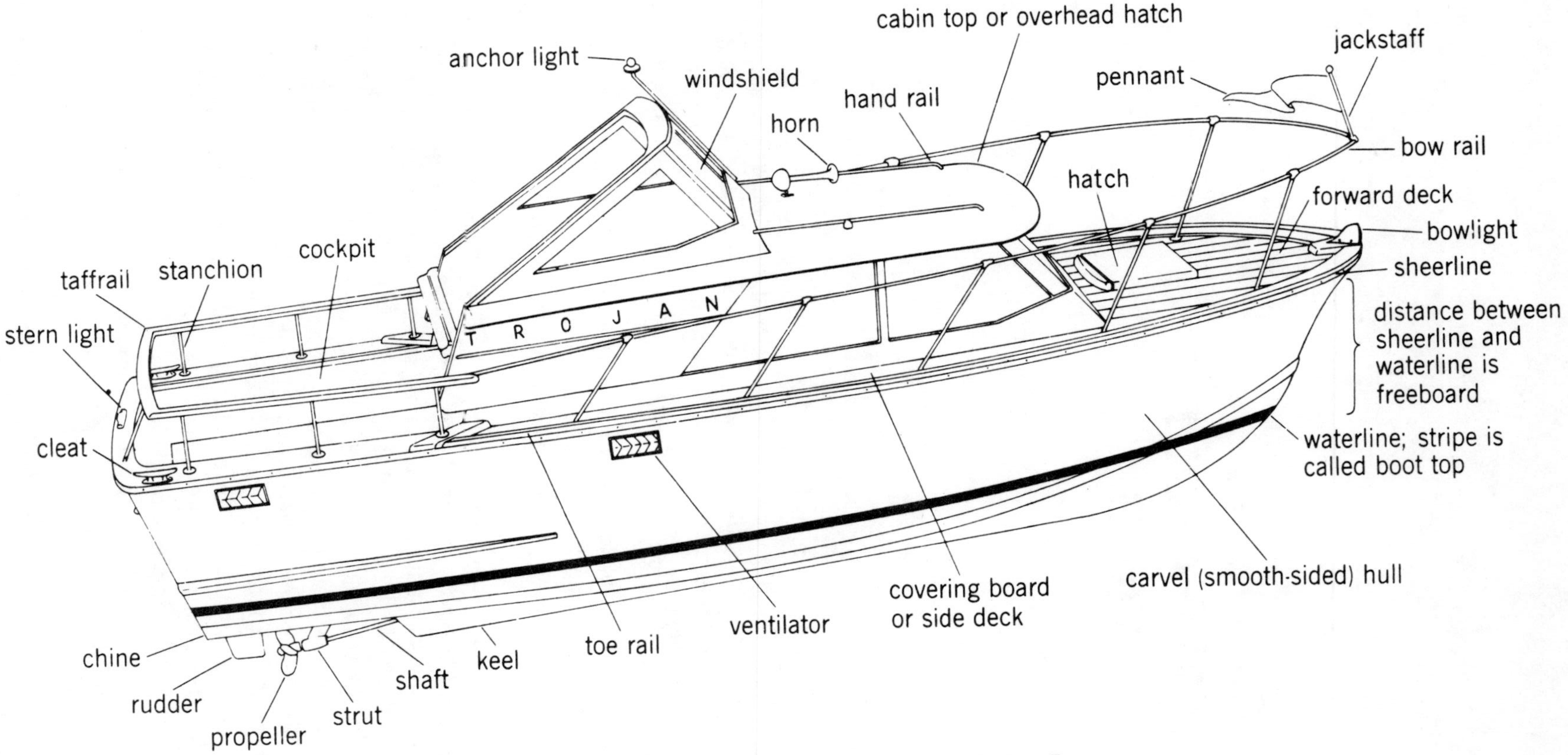

The parts of a powerboat. (*Courtesy Trojan Boat Company.*)

But note that only some of the terms are being discarded. Others, though crusty with age, have no substitute, or are shorter than their substitute, or are more easily said, learned, remembered. Aboard a boat, understanding, speed, and accuracy in communication are desirable and sometimes essential. The person who knows just where to fend off in response to your "Watch the starboard quarter" request is a greater asset than the person to whom you must say "Watch the back right side of the boat, the right side, that is, as you face forward." You may have smacked into the dock by then. The more critical the situation the greater is the need for clear, concise expression. That is why, if for no other reason, it is worth the effort to learn correct boating terminology. Use other words, by all means, when you discover they serve as well. I never object, though because of my training I sometimes wince, when "downstairs" is used for *below,* or "cabinet" for *locker* or "store" for *stow;* each seems to me to be as effective as the other. But when, for example, I am warned to "Look out for the driftwood over there" I invariably find myself wishing I had been told how many points the driftwood is off which bow. With precise advice I can respond quickly and safely.

Most of the terms you will find necessary to use concern parts of, and directional references to, the boat. Many of them have been used and explained elsewhere in this book. Together with the labeled illustration in this chapter, you have enough material from which to acquire a sound boating vocabulary. When you do, you will find that you also have a pretty fair notion of the nature and quality of the ideas the terms represent. You will be, in the best sense of the tag, a boatman. And ready for a bigger boat.

INDEX